James Starr Redfield

Redfield's Traveler's Guide to the City of New York

Vol. 1

James Starr Redfield

Redfield's Traveler's Guide to the City of New York
Vol. 1

ISBN/EAN: 9783337292409

Printed in Europe, USA, Canada, Australia, Japan

Cover: Foto ©Andreas Hilbeck / pixelio.de

More available books at **www.hansebooks.com**

TO THE

CITY OF NEW YORK

WITH A MAP.

NEW YORK
J. S. REDFIELD, *PUBLISHER*
140 FULTON STREET
1871.

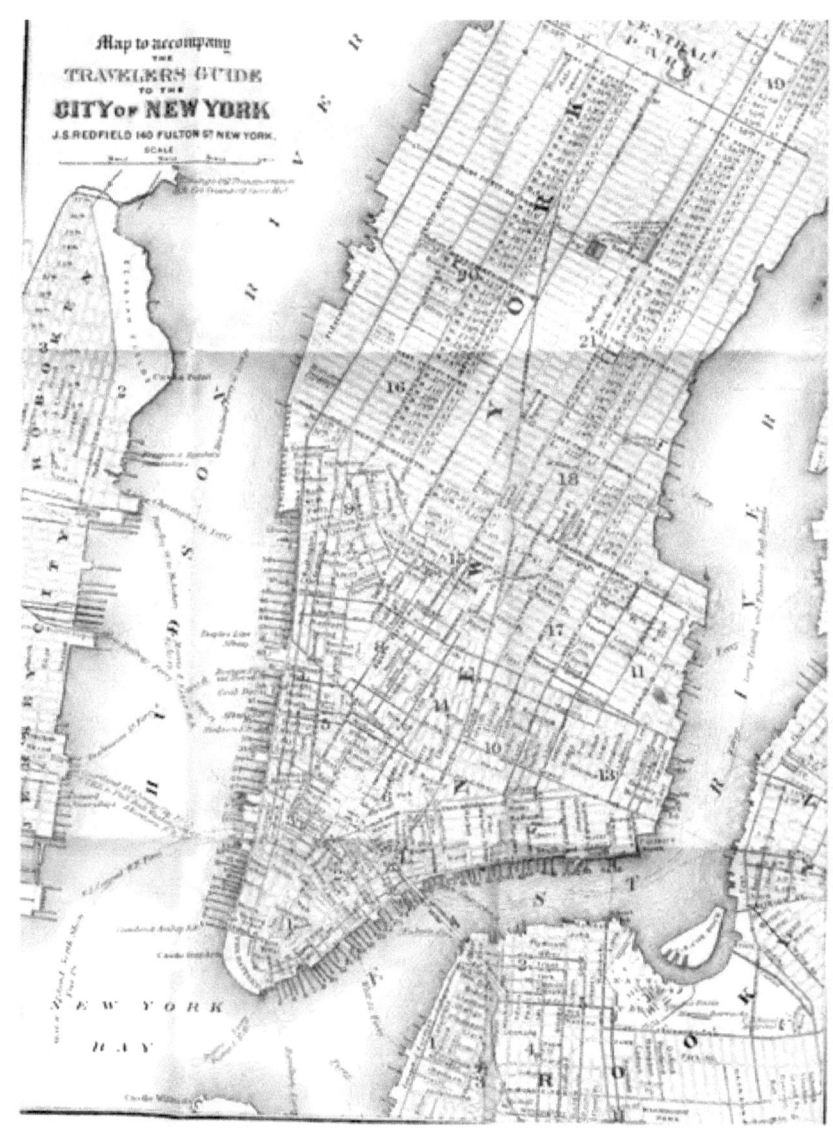

PREFACE.

A stranger who visits a metropolitan city for the first time, naturally feels no little anxiety as to how he shall avoid being surrounded by the land-sharks who will beset him on his arrival, and dog his footsteps in the city, if he should manifest the least evidence of being a stranger. He will also desire to know something of the comparative expense of living at the different hotels, boarding-houses, lodging-houses and restaurants, and where to find them. He will want to know where to find the principal churches, and where to look for the different places of amusement, the prices of admission, and how to reach them; where the public buildings worth seeing are located and the best way to get to them; where to look for picture galleries, libraries, colleges, public institutions, cemeteries, &c., &c., and where he shall find the finest drives around the city.

If he should be going abroad he will need all the information he can get about the different lines of steamers, and their rates of passage, letters of credit, passports, etc., etc., and all this information, and a great deal more, it is the purpose of this little book to give, in the most condensed manner, and at an inconsiderable cost.

NOTICE.

In collecting the various details of information contained in this little book, some imperfections and inaccuracies may be discovered when printed. New editions will be printed from time to time as they may be called for, and in every new edition corrections and additions will be made with the view of keeping it up with its date. The Publisher will be obliged therefore to any one who will point out errors or suggest improvements.

CONTENTS.

CHAPTER I.—*Preliminary Suggestions*—1. Baggage Express 2. Carriages. 3. Public porters. 4. Horse-car routes. 5. Omnibus routes. 6. Ferries. 7. Location of Piers. 8. Hotels. 9. Restaurants. 10. Boarding and Lodging-houses. 11. Table of distances in the city. 12. Telegraph offices.

CHAPTER II.—*Description of the City.*—1. Description of the city and harbor. 2. Historical sketch of the city. 3. Sanitary provisions. 4. Population—present and past.

CHAPTER III.—*Improvements in Progress.*—1. Improvements in Docks. 2. The Viaduct Railway. 3. The Brooklyn Bridge. 4. Union Railroad Passenger Depot.

CHAPTER IV.—*Public Parks and Squares.*—1. Central Park. 2. The Battery. 3. The Bowling Green. 4. City Hall Park. 5. Washington Square. 6. Tompkins Square. 7. Union Square. 8. Madison Square. 9. Mount Morris Square.

CHAPTER V.—*Public Buildings.*—1. Trinity Church. 2. The Post Office. 3. U. S. Treasury Building. 4. Custom House. 5. The City Hall. 6. The New Court House. 7. The Cooper Institute. 8. The National Academy of Design. 9. The Y. M. C. A. Building.

CHAPTER VI.—*Public Works.*—1. The Croton Aqueduct. 2. The Old Receiving Reservoir. 3. The New Receiving Reservoir. The Distributing Reservoir.

CHAPTER VII.—*Notable Streets and Sights.*—1. Broadway 2. Wall street. 3. Fifth avenue. 4. The Bowery. 5. The Five Points.

CHAPTER VIII.—*Places of Amusement.*—1. Booth's Theatre. 2. The Grand Opera House. The Academy of Music. 4. Wallack's. 5. Fifth Avenue Theatre. 6. Fourteenth Street Theatre. 7. Olympic. 8. The Globe. 9. Niblo's Garden. 10. Wood's Museum. 11. The Bowery Theatre. 12. The Stadt Theatre. 13. Union Square Theatre. 14. Lent's Circus.

CHAPTER IX.—*Drives.*—1. To Jerome Park. 2. To Kingsbridge. 3. To Fordham. 4. To Greenwood Cemetery. 5. To Coney Island. 6. To Staten Island.

CHAPTER X.—*Public Markets.*

CHAPTER XI.—*Public Libraries.*—1. The Astor Library. 2. The Mercantile Library. 3. The N. Y. Society Library. 4. Library of the N. Y. Historical Society. 5. Cooper Institute Library. 6. The Apprentice's Library. 7. The Law Library. 8. The City Library. 9. The Mott Memorial Library. 10. The Medical Library. 11. The Printers' Library. 12. The Women's Library. 13. Library of the Y. M. C. Association.

CHAPTER XII.—*Principal Churches.*

CHAPTER XIII.—Public Institutions.

CHAPTER XIV.—Picture Galleries and Artists' Studios.

CHAPTER XV.—*Principal Charitable Institutions.*—1. Institution for the Deaf and Dumb. 2. The Blind Asylum. 3. Bloomingdale Asylum for the Insane. 4. The Leake and Watts Orphan House. 5. N. Y. Orphan Asylum. 6. N. Y. Juvenile Asylum. 7. The Sailors' Snug Harbor. 8. The Five Points House of Industry.

CHAPTER XVI.—*Colleges—Literary and Medical.*—1. Columbia College. 2. N. Y. University. 3. College of the City of New York. 4. N. Y. College of Physicians and Surgeons. 5. University Medical College. 6. Bellevue Medical College. 7. N. Y. Medical College and Hospital for Women. 8. The Homœopathic Medical College. 9. Eclectic Medical College.

CHAPTER XVII.—*Principal Cemeteries in and around the City.*—1. Greenwood Cemetery. 2. Cypress Hills Cemetery. 3. Cemetery of the Evergreens. 4. Trinity Cemetery. 5. The Marble Cemetery in Second street. 6. Calvary Cemetery.

CHAPTER XVIII.—Departure of Coastwise and River Steamers and their Rates of Fare.

CHAPTER XIX.—Principal Railroad Stations and how to find them.

CHAPTER XX.—The Suburbs.

CHAPTER XXI.—*Foreign Travel.*—1. Passports. 2. List of Foreign Consuls residing in the City. Foreign steamers—their days of sailing, etc.

THE

TRAVELER'S GUIDE.

CHAPTER I.

PRELIMINARY.

1. Preliminary Suggestions.—2. Baggage Expresses.—3. Carriages.—4. Public Porters.—5. Horse-Car Routes.—6. Omnibus Routes.—7. Ferries.—8. Location of Piers.—9. Hotels.—10. Restaurants.—11. Boarding and Lodging-Houses.—12. Table of Distances.—13. Telegraph Offices.

§ 1. Preliminary Suggestions.

THE accounts which appear almost every day in the newspapers of the robbing of strangers on the steamers or cars, or just after landing in the city, ought to be seen and read, one would think, by almost every one, either in the city or country, yet to-morrow's "Tribune" or "Herald" will probably record the experience of another victim to these robberies. For the benefit, therefore, of those who do *not* read the papers, as well as of those who think themselves too "smart" to be caught by sharpers, we hereby inform them that on all the great lines of travel, either by rail or steamer, there are parties constantly traveling, educated to their profession, whose sole business it is to "fleece" the stranger in some way. They generally travel in companies of two or three, and when they club together to "do" a man, he will be smart indeed if they do n't accomplish their purpose. We deem it the first duty of a guide-book to warn the traveler to be at all times on his guard, and to help him, we recommend him to observe the following rules, strictly:

I. Never to play euchre or any other game of cards or chance with a stranger, either on the boat or cars.

II. Never make an exhibition of your money, nor let any one know you have any about your person.

III. Remember always that you are in danger from pickpockets. Think of it before starting out, and protect yourself accordingly.

IV. Never exchange your greenbacks for anybody's check, no matter how large a balance may *seem* to be in your favor.

V. Never exchange your greenbacks for gold (or what appears to be gold), *no matter how much distress the party may appear to suffer* who wants it.

VI. If you have money or valuables on your person and are obliged to be out over night in steamer or cars, get a state-room or section in sleeping car, at whatever cost, where you can lock out the thieves.

VII. If you have a state-room never leave it a moment unlocked.

VIII. Never buy a railroad or steamer's ticket from a stranger unless at a responsible ticket office.

IX. Never employ a hackman until you have seen the license number on his carriage and taken it down in your memorandum book.

X. If you have money or valuables about you when you arrive at your hotel, hand them over to the proprietor or to his representative, and take his receipt therefor.

XI. If you should be going abroad, go to some well-known and responsible bankers, and nowhere else, and get a draft or circular notes. Take no more gold and silver with you than you may need for pocket money.

XII. If you need *any* information about your route after you arrive in the city, ask it of a policeman, or at some respectable-looking store.

§ 2. Baggage Expresses.

The baggage express man is a comparatively modern institution. He is a sort of anxiety-saving machine; one which, for a small consideration, relieves the traveler from all care and thought about his baggage on his arrival. He travels on all the principal railroads and steamers (except foreign) bringing passengers to the city and it is his business to solicit your baggage checks, for which he will give you a receipt or check, which binds his employers, who are regarded as perfectly responsible, and he will get your baggage for you and deliver it at your residence or hotel, either in the city or any of its suburbs, or at any other depot or steamer, to which you may be going, at a stipulated time.

[That a piece of baggage might happen to get mislaid, or that some employee of the company might be careless and deliver a piece of baggage at the wrong place, or might not deliver it at the time promised, is among the probabilities, as every one must know, who has ever had anything to do with a large business like this; but as the success in business of these express companies depends upon the faithful performance of their promises, we think they will be found trustworthy; and in case of accident prompt to redress it.]

Relieved from the care of his baggage, and not inclined to walk, the traveler may step into an omnibus or horse-car—some one of which he will always find in the vicinity of the depot or landing—and proceed at once to his hotel or lodgings; he may have to ride on more than one route to reach his destination, but on inquiry the conductor will inform him whether he must change cars or route, and where.

The baggage express business is mainly done by two companies—*Dodd's* and *Westcott's*—who have offices in New York and Brooklyn.

Dodd's Express takes the baggage of the N. J. Central, the New Jersey and the New Haven Railroads; and of the following steamers: the Mary Powell, the People's Line, and the Stonington Line.

Dodd's Prices.

For delivering a piece of baggage anywhere in the city below 50th street	40
In Yorkville and Harlem	1 00
Brooklyn	50
Brooklyn from New Haven R.R.	60
Williamsburg	75
Jersey City and Hoboken	75

Westcott's Express takes the baggage of the Hudson River, the Harlem, the Delaware and Lackawanna, and the Morris and Essex Railroads.

Westcott's Prices.

Anywhere in the city below 40th street	40
Above 40th and not above 60th street	50
Yorkville and Harlem	75
Brooklyn or Williamsburg	50
Jersey City or Hoboken	75

The price is the same for taking a piece of baggage to the station or steamer as for delivering it.

On leaving the city or Brooklyn, the traveler can go to either of these baggage express offices and procure his railroad or steamer tickets, and have his baggage checked at his house or hotel to his destination, which will save him a vast deal of trouble. He of course pays the same for his ticket that he would pay at the steamer or depot, and the usual charge of the baggage express man who calls at the house or hotel and takes his baggage.

⁎ The Erie Railroad Company have a baggage express of their own. Travelers by that road may leave their checks at the office at the depot, and their baggage will be duly forwarded to them, at the foregoing rates.

N. B. The hack proprietors have recently formed an association among themselves, and agreed to a scale of prices to carry passengers, and to deliver baggage by an express, which they call the "Association Baggage Express." They deliver baggage for 25 cents each piece.

Their agents will be found at the various depots and landings, and wear Association badges on their hats. As they do not go on the cars or steamers, travelers who would employ them must retain their checks till they arrive.

§ 3. Carriages.

If the traveler have ladies with him and require a carriage, he will always find one at the depot or landing, without the trouble of hunting for it, and he will be subject to running a gauntlet through a bedlam which he will remember as long as he lives. To many travelers carriages are an indispensable convenience, and for the benefit of those who are obliged to employ them, we subjoin the legal rates of fare which licensed hackmen are allowed to charge. Each carriage is required to have its license number conspicuously painted on its lamps, and the legal rates of fare printed and posted up within it in plain sight; and no hackman whose carriage is not so furnished, can collect any fare from his customer. Any stranger who may be overcharged or otherwise outraged by a licensed hackman, can have his grievance promptly redressed by making his complaint at the office of the Mayor of the city at the City Hall. But particular care must be taken to report the correct number painted on the coach.

Fare for Hackmen, Coaches and Carriages.

1. For conveying a passenger any distance not exceeding one mile, fifty cents; for conveying two passengers the same distance, seventy-five cents, or thirty-seven and a half cents each; and for every additional passenger, thirty-seven and a half cents.

2. For conveying a passenger any distance exceeding a mile, and within two miles, seventy-five cents; and for every additional passenger, thirty-seven and a half cents.

3. For the use of a hackney coach or carriage, by the day, with one or more passengers, five dollars.

4. For the use of a hackney coach or carriage, by the hour, with one or more passengers, with the privilege of

going from place to place, and stopping as often as may be required, one dollar an hour.

5. In all cases where the hiring of a hackney coach or carriage is not, at the time thereof, specified to be by the day or hour, it shall be deemed to be by the mile.

6. For children between two and fourteen years of age, half price is only to be charged; and for children under two years of age, no charge is to be made.

7. Whenever a hackney coach or carriage shall be detained, excepting as aforesaid, the owner or driver shall be allowed at the rate of seventy-five cents an hour.

8. Every driver or owner of a hackney coach, carriage, or cab, shall carry, transport, and convey in and upon his coach, carriage, or cab, in addition to the person or persons therein, one trunk, valise, saddle-bag, carpet-bag, portmanteau, or box, if he be requested so to do, for each passenger, without charge or compensation therefor; but for every trunk or such other articles above named, more than one for each passenger, he shall be entitled to demand and receive the sum of six cents.

9. In case of disagreement as to distance or price, the same shall be determined by the Mayor.

10. The owner of any hackney coach or carriage shall not demand or receive any pay for the conveyance of any passenger, unless the number of the carriage, and the rates and prices of fare, shall be fixed and placed in the manner hereinbefore described.

11. The owner or driver of any hackney coach or carriage, shall not be entitled to receive any pay from any person from whom he shall have demanded any greater price or rates, than he may be authorized to receive as aforesaid.

12. No owner or driver of any hackney coach or carriage in the city of New York shall ask, demand, or receive any larger sum than he or they may be entitled to receive, as aforesaid, under the penalty of ten dollars for every such offence, to be sued for and recovered from the owner or owners, or driver of any such hackney coach or carriage, severally and respectively.

Some hackmen have recently formed an Association

among themselves, and agreed upon a tariff of prices which they say shall be uniform and permanent. Their runners will be found at the depots and landings, and may be known by their wearing the Association badges upon their hats. Their prices are fifty cents each for carrying passengers any distance between 27th street and the Battery; twenty-five cents additional if they go above 27th street. Baggage carried free of charge.

§ 4. Public Porters.

Sometimes a traveler has occasion for the services of a porter, either on his arrival, or during his stay in the city. We herewith give the legal rates he is entitled to charge.

1. For the carrying or conveyance of any article any distance within half a mile, twenty-five cents, if carried by hand; fifty cents if carried on a wheelbarrow or hand-cart; if the distance exceed half a mile, one half the above rates in addition thereto, and in the same proportion for any greater distance.

2. No public porter or hand-cartman shall be entitled to recover or receive any fare, from any person, for the transportation of any article or articles, unless he wears a badge with his name and the number of his license engraved thereon.

§ 5. Horse-Car Routes.

The fare on all the horse-car routes, with the following exceptions, is five cents. The Fourth Avenue road is six cents for any distance, and if you go above 34th street, it is eight cents. On the Third Avenue, the fare is six cents if you go above 65th street. On the Eighth Avenue, it is eight cents above 59th street, and ten cents above 72nd street. On the Second Avenue, if one goes above 63d street, the fare is six cents.

SECOND AVENUE.—*Peck Slip to Harlem.*—From Peck Slip to Bowery, *via* South, Oliver and Chatham streets, thence to Harlem, *via* Grand, Chrystie and Second Avenue. RETURN, *via* Second Avenue to East 23rd street, thence to Peck Slip, *via* East 23rd street, First Avenue, Allen and Grand streets, Bowery, Chatham and Pearl streets.

Cars run from 63rd street to Peck Slip and return, all night.
Last Car leaves 63rd street for Harlem at 12.30, A. M.
" " Harlem for 63rd street at 1, A. M.

THIRD AVENUE.—*Park Row to Harlem.*—Via Chatham street, Bowery and Third Avenue. RETURN, same route.
    Cars run all night.

FOURTH AVENUE AND HARLEM.—From Park Row to Centre, Grand, Bowery, Fourth Avenue to 42nd street, Madison Avenue to East 86th street; also from East 32nd street to Lexington Avenue, East 34th street, and Hunter's Point Ferry. RETURNING, same route to Park Row.
    Last car leaves 34th street Ferry at 10.50, P.M.
      "   "   Astor House at 11.30. P.M.
  Madison Avenue Branch.—Last car leaves Astor House at 7.30, P.M.
      "   "   East 86th street at 9, "

SIXTH AVENUE.—*From Astor House to Central Park.*—Via Vesey, Church and Chambers streets, West Broadway, Canal, Varick and Carmine streets and Sixth Avenue. RETURN, by same route, to Chambers street, thence *via* College Place and Vesey street, to corner Broadway. BRANCH diverges *via* Canal street to Broadway.
    Cars run all night on Astor House route.
  Canal street Branch.—Last car leaves 43rd street at 10.15, P.M.
      "   "   Canal and Broadway at 10.50, P.M.

SEVENTH AVENUE.—*From Astor House to Central Park.*—Via Barclay, Church and Chambers streets, West Broadway, Canal, Thompson, West 4th, Macdougal and 8th streets, Greenwich Avenue and Seventh Avenue to West 59th street. RETURN, by same route, to Chambers street, thence *via* College Place and Barclay street, to corner of Broadway.
    Last car leaves Central Park at 11, P.M.
      "   "   Broadway and Barclay at 11.45, P.M.

SEVENTH AVENUE AND BROADWAY.—*From Astor House to Central Park.*—Via Barclay, Church and Chambers streets, West Broadway, Greene street, Clinton Place, University Place, Broadway and Seventh Avenue, to West 59th street. RETURN, *via* same route, to University Place, thence *via* Wooster, Canal, West Broadway and Barclay streets, to corner Broadway. BRANCH diverges *via* Broome street to Broadway.
    Last car leaves Central Park at 11, P.M.
      "   "   Broadway and Barclay at 11.45, P.M.
  Broome St. Branch.—Last car leaves Central Park at 11, P.M.
      "   "   Broome St. and B'way at 11.30 P.M.

EIGHTH AVENUE.—*From Astor House to Manhattanville.*—Via Vesey, Church and Chambers streets, West Broadway, Canal and Hudson streets, and Eighth Avenue, to West 125th street. RETURN, *via* same route, to West Broadway, thence *via* College Place and Vesey street, to corner Broadway. BRANCH diverges *via* Canal street to Broadway.
    Cars run every 15 minutes all night on Astor House route.
  Canal street Branch.—Last car leaves 49th street Depot at 10.30, P.M.
      "   "   Canal and Broadway at 11, "

NINTH AVENUE.—*From Broadway and Fulton street to and up Ninth Avenue.*—Via Fulton and Greenwich streets and Ninth Avenue to West 54th street. RETURN, *via* Ninth Avenue, Greenwich, Gansevoort, Washington and Fulton streets, to Broadway.
    Last car leaves 54th street Depot at 9 P.M.
      "   "   Fulton and Broadway at 10 P.M.

TENTH AVENUE, OR WEST SIDE.—*From South Ferry to Central Park.*—*Via* Whitehall street, Battery Place, West street, Tenth Avenue, and West 59th street, to corner of Fifth Avenue. RETURN, by same route, to Battery Place, thence *via* State and Whitehall streets to South Ferry.

 Last car leaves 59th St. and Tenth avenue at 10.30 P.M.
  " " South Ferry, 11.30 P.M.

EAST SIDE.—*South Ferry to Grand street Ferry and to Central Park.*—*Via* Whitehall and Water streets, Old Slip, South and Corlears streets, to Grand street, thence *via* Grand, Goerck and Houston streets, Avenue D, East 14th street, Avenue A, East 23rd street, First Avenue and East 59th street, to corner Fifth Avenue. RETURN, *via* East 59th street, First Avenue, East 23rd street, Avenue A, East 14th street, Avenue D, Houston and Mangin streets, to Grand street, thence *via* Monroe, Jackson, Front, South, Front and Whitehall streets, to South Ferry.

 Last car leaves 59th street and Fifth avenue at 10.15 P.M.
  " " South Ferry at 11.15 P.M.

BLEECKER STREET AND FULTON FERRY.—*From Fulton Ferry to West Fourteenth Street, near Tenth Avenue* (GREEN LINE).—*Via* Fulton, William and Ann streets, Park Row, Chatham, Centre, Leonard, Elm, Howard, Crosby, Bleecker, Macdougal, West 4th, West 12th, Hudson, and West 14th streets. RETURN, *via* West 14th, Hudson, Bleecker, Crosby, Howard, Elm, Reade, Centre, Park Row, Beekman and South streets, to Fulton Ferry.

YELLOW LINE.—*Between same points.*—*Via* Fulton and Water streets, Peck Slip, and Pearl streets, New Bowery, Bowery, Canal, Elm, Howard, Crosby, Bleecker, Macdougal, West 4th, West 12th, Hudson and West 14th streets. RETURN, *via* West 14th, Hudson, Bleecker, Crosby, Howard, Elm and Canal streets, Bowery, New Bowery, Pearl and Ferry streets, Peck Slip, South and Fulton streets, to ferry.

 Last car leaves 14th street and Eleventh avenue at 12.30 P.M.
  " " Fulton Ferry at 1 A.M.

CROSS TOWN ROUTES.

Dry Dock and East Broadway Line.—*Via* Chatham street, East Broadway, Grand and Columbia streets, Avenue D, East 14th street, Avenue A. RETURN, *via* same route, to Avenue D, thence *via* 8th, Lewis and Grand streets, East Broadway, Chatham street and Park Row, corner Ann street.

 Last car leaves Avenue A and 14th street at 11.30 P.M.
  " " corner Broadway and Ann street at 12 P.M.

Park Row to Hunter's Point Ferry (East Thirty-fourth Street.)—*Via* Chatham street, East Broadway, Clinton street, Avenue B, East 14th street, Avenue A, East 23rd street, First Avenue, and East 34th street, to ferry. RETURN, *via* East 34th street, to depot, thence *via* Avenue B, Chatham street and Park Row, to corner Ann street.

 Last car leaves ferry, 34th street and E. R. at 11.15 P.M.
  " " corner Broadway and Ann street at 12 P.M.

Grand Street Ferry to Cortlandt Street Ferry.—*Via* Grand street, East Broadway, Canal, Walker, North Moore and Washington streets, to Cortlandt street. RETURN, *via* Cortlandt, Greenwich, Beach, Lispenard, Canal and Grand streets.

Last car leaves Grand street Ferry at 10 P.M.
" " Cortlandt street at 10.30 P.M.

Thirty-fourth and Desbrosses Streets Line.— Via First avenue, 23rd street, Avenue A, 14th street, Avenue D, Columbia street, Grand street, Sullivan street, Vestry street, Washington street, to Desbrosses street and ferry. RETURN, by same route to Grand, Lewis, Eighth, Avenue D, to starting point over same route.

Last car leaves 34th street at 10.30 P.M.
" " Desbrosses street at 11.20 P.M.

Grand Street Ferry to Desbrosses Street Ferry.— Via Grand, Sullivan, Vestry, Greenwich, and Desbrosses streets, to ferry. RETURN, *via* Desbrosses, Washington, Vestry, Sullivan and Grand streets, to ferry.

Last car leaves Grand street Ferry, E. R. at 11.40 P.M.
" " Desbrosses street and N. R. at 12.10 P.M.

Grand Street Ferry and Weehawken Ferry (Forty-second Street).— Via Grand, Goerck, East Houston and 2nd streets, Avenue A, East 14th street, Fourth Avenue, 23rd street, Broadway, West 34th street, Tenth Avenue, and West 42nd street, to ferry. RETURN. *via* West 42nd street, Tenth Avenue, West 34th street, Broadway, 23rd street, Fourth Avenue, East 14th street, Avenue A, Houston, Cannon, and Grand streets, to ferry.

Last car leaves Ferry, foot of 42nd street and N. R. at 11.30 P.M.
" " Grand street ferry, E. R. at 12.25 P.M.

Avenue C.—From Fourth Avenue, cor. East 42nd street to Lexington Avenue, 35th street, First Avenue, East 23rd street, Avenue A, East 17th street, Avenue C, Third street, First Avenue, East and West Houston to West and Chambers street ferries. RETURN, *via* West, Charlton, Prince, Stanton, Pitt, Avenue C, East 18th, Avenue A, East 23rd, First Avenue, East 36th, Lexington Avenue, to corner East 42nd, and Fourth Avenue.

Cars run from 5.30 A.M. to 12 P.M.

§ 6. Omnibuses.

From many portions of the city and, especially, from almost any part of Broadway, the omnibuses afford the readiest means of reaching the principal ferries to the suburbs of the city. The routes are always designated upon the outside of the coaches, and the stranger who takes the precaution to look before he leaps, never need make a mistake.

[The fare on all the omnibuses is 10 cents a ride—whatever the distance].

1. **Fifth Avenue and Fulton Ferry Line** (Blue Stages). Route, from cor. 43d st and 5th av., down the avenue to 12th st., to University pl., to 11th st., to Broadway, to Fulton st., and to the Ferry.

Last stage leaves 43rd street and Fifth avenue, at 11, P. M.
" " Fulton Ferry at 12, P. M.

2. **Madison Avenue and Wall St. Ferry Line.** Route, from 40th st. and Madison av. to Broadway, to Wall st., and to the Ferry.
  Last stage leaves 40th street and Madison avenue, at 10.15 P.M.
  " " Wall street Ferry, at 11.30 P.M.

3. **Fourth Avenue and Broadway Line.** Route, from 42d st. and 4th av., (New Union Depot,) down the avenue to Broadway, to South Ferry.
  Last stage leaves Union Depot, 42nd st. and Fourth avenue, at 10.30.
  " " South Ferry, at 11.30 P.M.

4. **Broadway, Twenty-third St. and Ninth avenue Line.** Route, from 30th st. (Hudson R. R. Depot) and 9th av. to 23d st., to Broadway, and to South Ferry.
  Every two minutes a stage leaves South Ferry for 30th st. Every eight minutes one leaves for Ferry foot of 23rd street.
  Last stage leaves 29th street and Ninth avenue, at 10.20.
  " " South Ferry, at 11.30 P.M.

5. **Broadway and Eighth St. Line.** Route, from foot of East 10th st. (Greenpoint Ferry), to 8th st., to Broadway, and to South Ferry.
  Last stage leaves foot East 10th street, Greenpoint Ferry, at 10.30.
  " " South Ferry, at 11.15 P.M.

6. **Broadway and Second St. Line.** Route, from foot of Houston st., E. R. (Williamsburg Ferry), to 2d st., to Bleecker st., to Broadway, to Cortlandt st., and to Jersey City Ferry.
  Last stage leaves Houston street Ferry, E. R., at 10 P.M.
  " " Cortlandt Ferry, at 10.45 P.M.

§ 7. Ferries.

Connecting the city with its suburbs:—

East River Side.

Astoria, from foot of 92d st. Fare, 4 cents.

Long Island City (late Hunter's Point), from James' slip every half hour. Fare, 6 cents.

———— From foot of 34th st., in the forenoon, every 15 minutes, in the afternoon, every 7 minutes. Fare, 4 cents.

[These ferries connect with the Long Island and Flushing Railroads.]

Greenpoint, from foot of 23d st. and 10th st., from 6 A.M. to 9 P.M., every 15 minutes. Fare, 4 cents.

Brooklyn, E. D. (Williamsburg), from foot of Houston st. to Grand st. Fare, 3 cents.

———— From foot of Grand st. to Grand st., and to South 7th st. Fare, 3 cents.

———— From foot of Roosevelt st. to South 7th st., from 5 A.M. to 8 P.M., every 10 minutes. Fare 3 cents.

[The South Side, L. I. Railroad depot is at South 7th street ferry.]

Brooklyn. From foot of New Chambers st. to Bridge st., Brooklyn, every 15 minutes, from 5 A.M. to 10 P.M. Fare 2 cents.

Brooklyn, UNION FERRY COMPANY. [Fare on all these ferries, 2 cents; 17 tickets for 25 cents. Between the hours of 5 and 7.30, morning and evening, the ferriage at all the ferries of this Company is *one cent.* Tickets good at all the Company's ferries.]

———— Catharine Ferry, from foot of Catharine st. to foot of Main st. from 5 A.M. to 9 P.M., every 10 minutes; from 9 P.M. to 12 P.M., every 20 minutes.

2*

Brooklyn, **Fulton Ferry**, from foot of Fulton st. to Fulton st., Brooklyn.

This is the principal Ferry between New York and Brooklyn. There are four boats employed from 7 A. M. to 7 P. M., and two are running all night. Trips during the day are made as rapidly as a boat can cross. From 7 P. M. to 12 P. M., trips are made every 12 minutes. from 2 P. M. to 7 A. M., every 15 minutes.

[At the landing on the Brooklyn side, more than a dozen different horse car routes have their termini. There is scarcely any part of Brooklyn which cannot be readily reached by one or the other of these cars. The stranger has only to inquire of the car-starter at the Ferry to ascertain which car he must take to reach his destination.]

—— Wall st. Ferry, from foot of Wall st. to Montague st., from 5 A.M. to 8 P.M., every 10 minutes; and every 20 minutes, from 8 P.M. to 12 P. M.

—— South Ferry, from foot of Whitehall st. to Atlantic st., from 5 A. M. to 11 P. M., every 12 minutes; from 11 P. M. to 5 A. M., every half hour.

—— Hamilton Avenue Ferry, from foot of Whitehall st. to Atlantic Dock, from 7 A M. to 6¼ P.M., every 10 minutes; from 6¼ P.M. to 9 P.M., every 15 minutes; from 9 P.M. to 7 A M., every half hour.

Harlem and Astoria, from Peck Slip at almost every hour in the day, stopping at Astoria. Fare, ten cents.

—— and Morrisiana, from Fulton Slip—east side—almost every hour in the day. Fare, 10 cents.

Bay Ridge, from foot of Wall st., six trips a day. Fare, 15 cents.

Staten Island, to Tompkinsville, Stapleton, and Vanderbilt's Landing, from foot of Whitehall st. every hour, from 6 A.M. to 9 P.M., and a last boat at 11:45 P. M. Fare 10 cents.

[This ferry connects with the Staten Island Railroad.]

North River Side.

Staten Island, North Shore, to New Brighton, Sailors' Snug Harbor, West Brighton, Port Richmond, and Elm Park, from pier 19, from 6 A.M. to 8 P.M., every hour, except at 1 P.M. Fare, 12 cents.

Jersey City, Communipaw, from foot of Liberty st. to N. J. Central R.R. every 20 minutes. Fare, 3 cents.

—— from foot of Cortlandt st. to foot of Montgomery st., from 7 A.M. to 10 P. M. every 10 minutes; from 10 to 12 P. M., every 15 minutes; from 12 P.M. to 4 A.M., every 30 minutes; from 4 to 7 A.M., every 15 minutes. Fare, 3 cents.

—— From foot of Desbrosses st. to same landing. Fare, 3 cents.

[These two ferries connect with the New Jersey Railroad.]

—— Long Dock (Pavonia), from foot of Chambers st., from 1 A.M. to 7 P.M., every 15 minutes; from 7 P.M. to 1 A.M., every half hour. Fare 3 cents.

—— Long Dock (Pavonia), from foot of 23d st. Fare, 3 cents.

[These ferries connect with the Erie, the Northern New Jersey, and the Hackensack Railroads.]

Hobcken, from foot of Barclay st.
—— From foot of Christopher st., from 5 A.M. to 8 P.M., every 15 minutes; from 8 to 12 P.M., every 20 minutes.
[These ferries connect with the Morris and Essex, the Delaware and Lackawanna, and the Bloomfield and Montclair Railroads.]
Bull's Ferry and Fort Lee, from pier 51. Fare, 12 cents.
Weehawken, from foot of 42d st., from 6 A.M. to 7 P.M., every 40 minutes. Fare, 12 cents.

§ 8. Location of Piers.

By reference to the following, the stranger who approaches the city by steamboat, or who is to leave it by the same means, will be able to ascertain, not only on which side of the city—whether E. R. or N. R.—but also, at the foot of what street the Pier to which he is to go may be found. Remembering of course that E. R. means East River, and N. R. North River.

North River.

No. 1, foot Battery pl.
" 2, 3, bet. Battery pl. and Morris
" 4, foot Morris
" 5, 6, 7, bet. Morris and Rector
" 8, foot Rector
" 9, 10, bet. Rector and Carlisle
" 11, foot Carlisle
" 12, foot Albany
" 13, bet. Albany and Cedar
" 14, foot Cedar.
" 15, foot Liberty
" 16, bet. Liberty and Cortlandt
" 17, 18, foot Cortlandt
" 19, bet Cortlandt and Dey
" 20, foot Dey
" 21, " Fulton
" 22, bet Fulton and Vesey
" 23, foot Vesey
" 24, bet Vesey and Barclay
" 25, foot Barclay
" 26, bet. Barclay and Robinson
" 27, foot Robinson
" 28, " Murray
" 29, " Warren
" 30, " Chambers
" 31, " Duane
" 32, bet. Duane and Jay

No. 33, foot Jay
" 34, " Harrison
" 35, " Franklin
" 36, " N. Moore
" 37, " Beach
" 38, " Hubert
" 39, " Vestry
" 40, " Watts
" 41, " Hoboken
" 42, " Canal
" 43, " Spring
" 44, bet. Spring and Charlton
" 45, foot Charlton
" 46, " King
" 47, " W. Houston
" 48, " Clarkson
" 49, " Leroy
" 50, " Morton
" 51, " Christopher
" 52, " W. 10th
" 53, " Charles
" 54, " Perry
" 55, " Hammond
" 60, " W. 18th
" 61, " W. 17th
" 62, " W. 18th
" 63, " W. 19th

East River.

No. 1, 2, foot Whitehall
" 3, " Moore
" 4, bet. Moore and Broad
" 5, bet. Broad and Coenties slip
" 6, 7, 8, Coenties slip
" 9, 10, bet. Coenties and Old slips
" 11, 12, Old slip
" 13, bet. Old slip and Gouverneur lane
" 14, foot Jones lane
" 15, 16, foot Wall
" 17, foot Pine
" 18, " Maiden lane
" 19, " Fletcher
" 20, 21. foot Burling slip
" 22, foot Fulton
" 23, " Beekman
" 24, bet. Beekman and Peck slip
" 25, 26, foot Peck slip
" 27, foot Dover
" 28, bet. Dover and Roosevelt
" 29, foot Roosevelt
" 30, bet. Roosevelt and James slip
" 31, 32, foot James slip
" 33, foot Oliver
" 34, 35, foot Catharine sl'p
" 36, bet. Catharine slip and Market

No. 37, 38, foot Market
" 39, bet. Market and Pike
" 40, 41, foot Pike
" 42, bet. Pike and Rutgers
" 43, 44, foot Rutgers
" 45, bet. Rutgers and Jefferson
" 46, foot Jefferson
" 47, bet. Jefferson and Clinton
" 48, foot Clinton
" 49, bet. Clinton and Montgomery
" 50, foot Montgomery
" 51, 52, foot Gouverneur
" 53, foot Jackson
" 54 " Corlears
" 55 " Cherry
" 56, 57, foot Broome
" 58, 59, " Delancey
" 60, foot Rivington
" 61, bet. Rivington and Stanton
" 62, foot Stanton
" 63, " E. Houston
" 64, " Fifth
" 65, " Sixth
" 66, " Seventh
" 67, " Eighth
" 68, " Ninth
" 69, " E. 10th
" 70, " E. 11th

§ 9. Hotels.

The first-class Hotels of New York city have long enjoyed the reputation of being the best in the world. They are numerous and well distributed throughout the city, and oftentimes occupy structures which are architectural ornaments to the city. They are spacious, some of them having a capacity to accommodate four or five hundred guests—and sumptuously furnished and supplied with every appointment which can in any way contribute to the comfort of the guest. Many of the hotels have adopted the European plan of charging separately for rooms and meals, others adhere to the old time American custom of including both items under one head. We subjoin a list of some of the hotels of each class, with their charges, in order that the traveler who desires to count the cost beforehand may have an opportunity of doing so. Some travelers prefer one plan and some the other.

Numerous and spacious as the hotels of the city are, there are seasons of the year when they are crowded, and when it is extremely difficult for a stranger arriving at night, especially—who has not engaged his room beforehand—to find sleeping accommodations. Persons visiting the city between the middle of August and the middle of October, will do well to take heed.

At the following hotels the prices named include rooms and meals.

Fifth Avenue Hotel, corner 23rd street and Fifth avenue. Charges $5 per day. Suites of rooms are extra.
St. Nicholas Hotel, Broadway and Spring street, $5 per day. Suites of rooms extra.
Clarendon Hotel, corner of Fourth avenue and 18th street. $5 per day. Suites of rooms extra.
Metropolitan Hotel, 582 Broadway. $4.50 per day. Suites extra.
New York Hotel, Broadway, from Washington to Waverley Place. $4 per day. Suites extra.
Prescott House, North-west corner of Broadway and Spring street. $4 per day. Suites extra.
Sturtevant House, 1186 Broadway. $3.50 per day.
Ashland House, corner of Fourth avenue and 24th street. $5 per day.
Union Square Hotel, Union Square. $3 per day.
Merchants' Hotel, 35, 37, 39 and 41 Cortlandt street. $3 per day.
Western Hotel, 9, 11, 13 and 15 Cortlandt street. $3 per day.

*** As a general thing at the principal hotels, breakfast may be had until 10 or 11 A.M. Dinner from 2 to 7 P.M., and Supper from 9 to 12 P.M.

Hotels conducted on the European plan. Up-town.

The *Brevoort House*, corner of 8th street and Fifth avenue. Bachelor's rooms, $2 per day and upwards. Suites $12 per day and upwards.
Madison Square Hotel, corner of Broadway and 21st street, Bachelor's rooms, $2 per day and upwards. Suites extra.
Hoffman House, corner Broadway and 24th street. Bachelor's rooms, $2 per day and upwards. Suites from $5 to $20.
St. James Hotel, corner Broadway and 26th street. Bachelor's rooms, $2 per day and upwards. Suites from $5 to $15.
Colman House, Broadway corner of 27th street. Bachelor's rooms, from $1 per day upwards. Suites $5 and upwards.
The Gilsey House, Broadway corner of 27th street. Bachelor's rooms, $2 and upwards. Suites extra.

Grand Central, 671 Broadway. Rooms from $2 upwards.

Grand Hotel. Broadway between 29th and 30th sts. Bachelor's rooms $1.50 and upwards. Suites, $8 and upwards.

Everett House, North-west corner of 17th street and Fourth avenue Bachelor's rooms, $1.50 per day and upwards.

Westmoreland Hotel, South-west corner of 17th street and Fourth avenue. Bachelor's rooms from $1 upwards. Suites from $5 to $10.

St. Denis Hotel, corner of Broadway and 11th street. Bachelor's rooms $1 and upwards. Suites extra.

Brandreth House, cor. Broadway and Canal st. Rooms from $1 to $5.

Down town.

The Astor House, Broadway, from Vesey to Barclay streets, Bachelor's rooms from $1 to $5. Suites $10.

United States Hotel, corner of Fulton and Water streets. Rooms from $1 upwards.

National Hotel, 3, 5 and 7 Cortlandt st. Rooms from $1 to $5 per day.

Cosmopolitan Hotel, corner of Chambers and West Broadway. Bachelor's rooms $1 per day. Double rooms $4.

Sweeney's Hotel, cor. Chatham and Duane sts. Rooms $1 to $3 per day.

French's Hotel, corner of Chatham and Frankfort streets. Rooms $1 and $1.50 per day.

Park Hotel, cor. Beekman and Nassau sts. Rooms $1 and $1.50 per day.

Belmont Hotel, 135 Fulton street. Rooms 50 cents to $1 per day.

§ 10. Restaurants.

If the number of people in the City of New York—strangers and citizens—who eat at least one meal a day every day at some eating-house could be arrived at, the figures, we apprehend, would startle the most indifferent inquirer. From the purlieus of the markets, where many a poor fellow makes a square meal on twenty-five cents—and even less— all the way up through the different grades of eating-houses till you arrive at Delmonico's where a man may, if he choose, pay $25 for a meal, the stranger will find the tables in all of them filled with crowds of people for five or six hours during the middle of the day, and some of them equally crowded from daylight in the morning till a late hour at night. The quality of the fare, as well as the prices, will be found to vary considerably.

It is rare to find two persons equally well pleased with the same place; we, therefore, abstain from recommending any particular houses, and have no hesitation in saying that there are, probably, hundreds of eating-houses quite as good as those we have named. The only way for a stranger to do is to try till he is suited.

We give, herewith, the address of a few of the restaurants where the stranger will find good fare; and, among them, will be found those of different nationalities, where the foreigner will find dishes served as he has been accustomed to have them at home—probably at a somewhat higher price, however.

DELMONICO'S, No. 2 S. William st., No. 22 Broad st., Corner Broadway and Chambers st., and Cor. of Fifth av. and 14th st.
MAILLARD, No. 619 Broadway.
BANG, HENRY J., Nos. 231 and 393 Broadway.
RUDOLPH'S, Nos. 162 and 411 Broadway.
NASH & FULLER, No. 40 Park Row.
SUTHERLAND, JNO., No. 64 Liberty st.
D. H. GOULD, No. 35 Nassau st.
SMITH & GREENE, No. 14 Cortlandt st., and 14 Beekman st.
JOHN H. CURRIER, No. 144 Fulton st.
ANTONIO LUCETTI, No. 1383 Broadway.
EMANUEL SOLARI, No. 44 University pl.
HENRY MOUQUIN, No. 141 Fulton st.
LOUIS HECKMAN, No. 122 William st.
ATLANTIC GARDEN (German), next door to Bowery Theatre.
FRANCESCO MARTINELLI, No. 49 Third av. (Italian restaurant, much frequented by artists), Table d'hote, 6 P. M. Prices moderate.

Lovers of good oysters would scarcely forgive us, if we did not give the address of the celebrated Fulton Market oyster house which is

DORLON & SCHAFFER, No. 243 and 244 Fulton Market.

§ 11. Boarding and Lodging Houses.

The stranger who may wish to locate himself in lodgings, or in a boarding house, is recommended to take a little time to look about him—going first to a hotel—and not make choice of a house until after a personal examination, or upon the recommendation of a friend. The number of lodging and boarding houses in the city is legion; many of them are all that can be desired, and others—are not. We do not propose to give a list, but we can assure the stranger that, in a very large number of these houses, he may live as comfortably as at a hotel, and at very considerably less expense.

Bachelors may find hall-bedrooms, with board, from $8 per week, upward—larger rooms in proportion—and a gentleman and his wife will find accommodation from $20 per week, upward.

§ 12. Table of Distances.

FROM THE BATTERY Miles.	FROM THE CITY HALL Miles.	TO	FROM THE BATTERY Miles.	FROM THE CITY HALL Miles.	TO
¼		Rector st.	6¼	5½	88th st.
½		Fulton.	6½	5¾	93d.
¾		Warren.	6¾	6	97th.
1	¼	Leonard.	7	6¼	102d.
1¼	½	Canal.	7¼	6½	107th.
1½	¾	Spring.	7½	6¾	112th.
1¾	1	Houston.	7¾	7	117th.
2	1¼	4th st.	8	7¼	121st.
2¼	1½	9th.	8¼	7½	126th.
2½	1¾	14th.	8½	7¾	130th.
2¾	2	17th.	8¾	8	136th.
3	2¼	24th.	9	8¼	140th.
3¼	2½	29th.	9¼	8½	145th.
3½	2¾	34th.	9½	8¾	150th.
3¾	3	38th.	9¾	9	154th.
4	3¼	44th.	10	9¼	159th.
4¼	3½	49th.	10¼	9½	164th.
4½	3¾	54th.	10½	9¾	169th.
4¾	4	58th.	10¾	10	174th.
5	4¼	63d.	11	10¼	179th.
5¼	4½	68th.	11¼	10½	183d.
5½	4¾	73d.	11½	10¾	188th.
5¾	5	78th.	11¾	11	193d.
6	5¼	83d.			

§ 13. Telegraph Offices.

TELEGRAPH OFFICES, (Domestic).—Most travelers have frequent occasion to use the telegraph, and they will find branch offices at nearly every hotel in the city, and at the various railroad depots.

TELEGRAPH OFFICES, (Foreign).—Atlantic and Pacific Telegraph Company's Offices: Produce Exchange, 31 and 33 Broadway; No. 2 Astor House; No. 60 Wall street; No. 11 Broad street; corner Broadway and Howard street; corner Broadway and 42nd street; and at 1278 Broadway.

CHAPTER II.
NEW YORK—DESCRIPTIVE AND HISTORICAL.

1. Description of the City and Harbor.—2. Historical Sketch of the City.—3. Sanitary Provisions.—4. Population of the City, Past and Present.

§ 1. Description of the City and Harbor.

NEW YORK City, the commercial metropolis of the New World, is situated on Manhattan Island, at the confluence of the Hudson and East Rivers, in Lat. 42°, 42′, 42″ west from Greenwich. This city enjoys by Nature, almost every advantage that could be desired to build up a great emporium. Its chartered limits embrace the entire island, and are of the same extent as those of the county, running from the Battery at the south point of the Island, north to Kingsbridge, a distance of thirteen and a half miles—with an average breadth of something less than two miles. Its greatest width is about 88th st., where it is two and a half miles wide. It is bounded on the north by the Harlem River, or Strait, which in its western portion was called, by the Dutch, Spuyten Duyvil Creek, on the east by the East River, or Strait, which separates it from Long Island, on the south by the harbor, and on the west by the Hudson or North River, which separates it from New Jersey. The width of the Hudson River is here quite uniform, being something more than a mile; while that of the East River varies, in some places being not more than two-fifths of a mile.

The city is connected with the main land on the north by several bridges; and with Long Island, New Jersey, and Staten Island by numerous ferries. The harbor is spacious and commodious, and has a circuit of not less than twenty-five miles. Its shores are covered with variegated scenery and numerous villages, and it embraces several beautiful islands. It is of easy entrance, and has sufficient capacity to accommodate the entire navies of the whole world. Dense forests of masts, bearing the flags of all nations, are crowded around the wharves of the city and its suburbs. The currents of the rivers are, at all times, very strong; keeping the harbor open in the winter sometimes when other harbors farther south are frozen. In very severe winters, the East River is occasionally obstructed for a short time at high tide by the ice, sufficiently to suspend navigation.

There is, besides, an outer harbor extending from the Narrows to Sandy Hook, on which point is a lighthouse eighteen miles from the city. At the bar, here, there are twenty-seven feet of water at high tide, and twenty-one feet at low tide. At the wharves of the city the tide rises and falls between four and five feet.

The inner harbor may also be entered by the way of Long Island Sound; and, it is almost certain that, when the obstructions, now being removed at Hell Gate, shall be entirely swept away, some of the European lines of steamers will come to the city by the way of the Sound, and have their landing at or above 86th st.—and it is quite possible that, whoever lives to see the new century come in, will see the commercial centre of the city on the upper end of the Island.

The islands within the harbor are Governor's, Bedloe's, and Ellis's Islands, which are all fortified—in a very antique manner however — and Blackwell's, Ward's, and Randall's Islands in the East River. At the Narrows (a strait which separates Long Island from Staten Island), is Fort Lafayette; and, opposite to this, on the Long Island shore, is Fort Hamilton—a modern-built fortress. The width of the Narrows is less than a mile. On the Staten Island shore are Forts Tompkins and Richmond: modern-built fortresses of considerable strength. The entrance to the harbor by the way of Long Island Sound is defended by Fort Schuyler at Throgg's Point, and Fort Wadsworth at Willett's Point.

The city is accessible also from the sea, by the way of the Kills; a strait which separates Staten Island from the New Jersey shore, and connects the waters of Raritan Bay with those of New York harbor.

The Island was, originally, very rocky and uneven—a ledge of rocks running from the south point to the north and branching off in various directions culminated, finally, at Washington Heights. These ridges are composed of primitive gneiss mixed with granite, hornblende, slate, and mica—all bearing evidence of violent upheaval. The dip of strata varies from 10° to 60°; the ranges being frequently broken laterally. The southern part of the Island and the shores in some places are alluvial sand-beds. The few swampy places are rapidly disappearing before the march of the man who opens and grades the new streets. Those who remember the old skating-ponds on the "Collect," and where Canal st. is to-day, will realize some of these changes.

Owing to the natural shape of the island, to the fact that it was first settled at its southern extremity, and to the eligibility of that section for the purposes of trade and commerce, it has resulted that the growth of the city has, with successive years, been manifested by a large increase of houses and stores in a northerly direction. In the business portion of the city, the number of dwelling-houses has decreased, yearly; the old houses suffering demolition, and their places being occupied by new and elegant warehouses. Therefore, in this lower section of the city, the number of inhabitants instead of increasing, or even remaining stationary, has decreased—while the northern section is rapidly increasing in numbers. The projected Viaduct Railroad will afford facilities for a rapid transit from the upper end of the Island to the City Hall Park, and then this change will become still more noticeable.

The general plan of the city is regular. In the old or southern part, now almost wholly devoted to business, the principal streets were generally laid out to conform to the shape of the Island, and hence its plan is not continuously uniform; although each of its large divisions is comparatively regular. The uniform plan of avenues and streets begins at Houston street—one mile above the City Hall. Above this point, the Island is divided longitudinally by parallel avenues 100 feet wide, which are crossed by streets numerically designated, and generally eighty feet wide—in most cases, running from river to river. A few of these streets are 100 feet wide.

The following graphic picture of some of the striking features of the city is from the pen of Mayor Hall, who, in his annual message to the Common Council, says:—

"New York Island has an area of twenty-two square miles and twenty-nine miles of water front, about three-fourths of which stretches along the Hudson and East Rivers, and the remaining one-fourth upon the Harlem River and Spuyten Duyvil Creek. The streets, roads, and avenues measure 460 miles. 291 miles of these are paved; 169 miles are unpaved. 19,000 gas-lights are burned every night at the public expense to light this area, water front, and extent of streets. Beneath the surface of the city, there are 340 miles of Croton-water pipes and 275 miles of sewers. If we accept the last Federal census, the number of our constituents is 942,-252. 1000 horse railway cars, 267 omnibuses, about 1,200 licensed vehicles, and quite as many more private vehicles continually traverse the thoroughfares, and subject them to increasing wear. It is claimed that 40,000 horses are constantly stabled or used within the city limits. On the 26th day of May last, relieving officers of the ordinance squad, stationed on Broadway, opposite the City Hall, were instructed to report the number of vehicles that, from 7 o'clock A. M. until 7 o'clock P. M., passed and repassed; and they reported 16,246, exclusive of omnibuses. These specimen statistics imply how great a city we have to care for, keep in repair, sustain by taxation, protect by policemen, firemen, or sanitary regulations, and make provision for, in respect to its more important future. During the ten months preceding May 1st, 1871, $284,000,000 worth of foreign merchandise, exclusive of specie, was imported into this city. During the same period, New York City paid the government $120,000,000 for duties on imports, and the value of exports, exclusive of specie, was $251,000,000.

"Certain peculiarities of the city and its people may be serviceably recalled. New York is the cosmopolitan city of the globe. People of all nationalities, many jealousies, and diverse creeds inhabit it. Every good and bad habit of human nature is illustrated within its limits. Every development of misfortune, poverty, vice, and crime is here to be found. To the evil manifestations, as well as the excellent ones of our city life, every clime contributes. It is a misfortune to New York population that, contributed to as it is by all parts of the world, local pride develops within our city under increasing difficulty. Every other city seems to have its pulpit and its citizens more prone from motives of local loyalty, if not to apologize for, or screen, at least to act kindly toward the defects and faults of fellow-citizens and rulers. Topographically, our city is peculiar; because it is long and narrow, and lacks circumference of immediate rural suburbs. The suburbs are really tributary cities divided from New York by wide rivers. Nearly sixty per cent. of the daily business inhabitants of New York own or rent their residences in the adjoining country; and, while their wives and children are practically under the government of other cities and counties, and even States, the business interests and security of person and property of the family men are practically under the government of New York City— and they are more impressed to blame where they have no domestic interests. Thus, while the city possesses, as will be inferred from many of the foregoing references, great advantages for development of commerce and wealth, other references imply how difficult it is to frame, and how vexatious it is for rulers to try and develop, a perfect or universally acceptable municipal government."

§ 2. Historical Sketch of the City.

The following succinct historical sketch of the city we quote from "Appleton's Cyclopedia," vol. xii., page 284, *et seq.*

"Henry Hudson discovered Manhattan island, Sept. 12, 1609. A temporary settlement was made by the Dutch in 1612, and a permanent one in 1623, when a small fort was built. The same year the first white child was born in the colony, Sarah Rapalje. Peter Minuits, the first Dutch governor, arrived in 1626, and purchased Manhattan island of the Indians for $24. A new fort was begun in 1633, on the present site of the Battery.

Wouter van Twiller became governor in 1633, and William Kieft in 1638. Tobacco was cultivated and slavery introduced before 1638. In 1644 a city hall was built in Coentics slip, and in 1647 Gov. Stuyvesant arrived; he was the last of the Dutch governors, ruling for 17 years. In 1653 a wall was built across the island at Wall street, for defence against Indians and the expected troops of Cromwell. In 1656, the city had 120 houses and 1,000 inhabitants. Wharfs were built in 1658, and a windmill in 1662. Charles II., having come to the English throne, assumed the Dutch occupancy in North America to be a usurpation, and on March 12, 1664, granted the entire territory to his brother the duke of York. A small fleet arrived in August, and the city surrendered without resistance, Col. Richard Nicolls assuming the office of governor. The name (New Amsterdam) was changed to New York, and an English form of government was established, which lasted 9 years; when, in July, 1673, the Dutch recaptured the city, named it New Orange, made Anthony Colve governor, and drove out the English. Their triumph was short, for by the peace between England and the states-general, the city was restored to the British crown, and once more called New York, and the Dutch power was finally ended, Nov. 10, 1674. For the remainder of the 17th century, the progress of the city was rapid. The old Dutch charter was replaced in 1686 by a more particular and liberal grant from the crown known as the Dongan charter. The only untoward event of the period was the unsuccessful rebellion of Jacob Leisler in 1689. At the close of the century, New York had about 750 dwellings, and 4,500 white and 750 black inhabitants. The first Trinity church was built in 1696. In 1702 a pestilent fever was brought from St. Thomas, from which nearly 600 persons died, or about 1 in 10 of the population. Some Huguenot families arrived, and, in spite of the state, freedom of religion was practically secured. Wall and other streets were paved, watchmen employed, and in 1711 a regular slave market was established. In 1719 the first Presbyterian church was built. The 'New York Gazette,' the fifth newspaper in the colonies, was begun in 1725, and Zenger's 'Weekly Journal' in 1733. Stages ran to Boston in 1732, being 14 days on the journey, and infectious fever prevailed with great fatality. In 1735 occurred the first attack upon the freedom of speech. By the death of Gov. Montgomerie, the duties of the office devolved until the appointment of a new governor upon Rip van Dam, the oldest member of the council. Van Dam officiated a year, when Gov. Cosby arrived, and claimed half the fees collected by Van Dam. A suit followed; and by the suppression of almost all the forms of justice, Van Dam was beaten. The people took up the quarrel, which was really the first step of separation or distinction between the people of Great Britain and those of the colony; lampoons, satires, and libellous ballads were rife, and the two newspapers joined in the controversy — the 'Gazette' supporting Cosby and the 'Journal' violently opposing him. The council directed certain copies of the 'Journal' to be burned, and ordered the mayor and magistrates to attend the ceremony; they refused, and the general assembly sympathized with them. Zenger was imprisoned for libel, and Cosby's party strained every nerve to convict him, going so far as to dismiss from the bar eminent lawyers who took his part. Against this, and in the face of the most outrageous rulings of the court, a jury declared Zenger not guilty. The year 1741 was remarkable for fire, pestilence, and insurrection; the Dutch church in the fort and a part of the fort itself were burned; yellow fever prevailed to a considerable extent; and the imaginary negro plot occurred. This so-called plot, which was never proved, created the greatest alarm; the fire in the fort was charged to the negroes; arrests were made, and upon the testimony of a single servant girl a number were executed. The most important victim was John Ury, a Roman Catholic priest, doubtless perfectly innocent, who was hanged in August. Within 6 months 154 negroes and 20 whites were imprisoned, of whom 55 were convicted, 78 confessed, 13 negroes were burned at the stake, 20 were hanged, 78 were transported, and the remainder were discharged. The evidence in any of the cases would now be considered worthless. In 1743 a pestilence carried off 217 persons, chiefly from marshy localities. In 1750 a theatre was established. In 1755 St. Paul's church was built. In that year began the stamp act excitement, and a colonial congress assembled in New York; figures of the governor and the devil holding the stamp act were burned in public. In 1765 the sons of liberty were organized to oppose the stamp act, a committee was appointed to correspond with other colonies, and the governor was burned in effigy. In 1770 a meeting of 3,000 citizens was held, who resolved not to submit to oppression, and a slight collision with the troops occurred; a committee of 100 was appointed to resist the importation of obnoxious goods, subsequently restricted to tea only; the statue of George III. in the Bowling Green was destroyed, and a marble statue erected to Pitt, for his exertions in the repeal of the stamp act. In 1772, Pitt having become Lord Chatham and changed his course, this statue was mutilated; it was removed in 1788, and the torso is now at a hotel in West Broadway. In 1773 the vigilance committee agreed to resist the landing of tea, and in 1774 a ship thus laden was stopped at Sandy Hook and sent back to England, 18 chests secretly landed being destroyed. The same year, at a great meeting on the common, strong revolutionary resolutions were passed. On April 3, 1775, the colonial assembly finally adjourned; on July 25, delegates were elected to the continental congress; and on Aug. 23 congress ordered Capt. Lamb to remove the cannon from the city forts to the highlands; resistance was offered from the Asia man-of-war, but 21 pieces, all that were mounted, were secured. On Aug. 26, 1776, by the result of the battle of Long Island, the city fell into the hands of the British, and so remained until the close of the war. On Sept. 21, 1776, a fire destroyed 493 houses, all the west side of Broadway from Whitehall to Barclay street (one eighth of the city) being laid in ashes. On Aug. 7, 1778, another fire destroyed 300 buildings around Cruger's wharf, on the East river. The winter of 1780 was very cold; ice covered the bay, and heavy teams and artillery crossed to Paulus Hook

(Jersey City). On Nov. 25, 1783, the British finally evacuated the city, and Gen. Washington marched in; the day is still annually celebrated under the name of Evacuation Day. During the war the British had nearly destroyed all the churches except the Episcopal, making prisons, riding schools, and stables of them; the college and schools had been closed. In 1785 the first federal congress organized at the city hall on the corner of Wall and Nassau streets; the next year the first Roman Catholic church (St. Peter's, Barclay street) was built, and the first divorce suit was brought. The adoption of the federal constitution was grandly celebrated in 1788; and the inauguration of President Washington took place at the city hall, April 30, 1789. In 1788 a serious riot occurred at the hospital, in consequence of the careless exposure of dissected bodies. The doctors were mobbed, their houses invaded, some of them were compelled to fly from the city, and others took refuge in the gaol. A census in 1790 showed a population of 29,906. In 1791 yellow fever carried off 200 victims. The city now just reaching the lower corner of the park, began to extend along the Boston road (Bowery) and Broadway; an almshouse was built in the park, and had 622 inmates in 1795. The park theatre was begun this year and opened in 1789. In the latter year 2,086 persons died in 3 months from yellow fever, which returned at intervals until 1805, but with diminished virulence. The Manhattan company, for supplying the city with water, was chartered in 1799. On Sept. 20, 1803, the corner stone of the city hall was laid by Mayor Livingston; the hall was finished in 1812, when the old one in Wall street was sold. In the winter of 1804, 40 stores in Wall and Front streets were burned. The free school society, the germ of the present board of education, was incorporated in 1805. The city had now 78,770 inhabitants, and streets were extending across the Canal street marsh, while the collect or swamp where the city prison now stands was being filled up. The spread the population was stimulated by the yellow fever, which drove a third of the people from their dwellings below the park to the woods and fields north of the fresh water. In 1807

Robert Fulton navigated the first steamboat from near New York to Albany. In 1812 Fulton leased the Brooklyn ferries for $4,000 a year to run by steam. A great fire in Chatham street in 1811 consumed nearly 100 houses. The war of 1812 with Great Britain temporarily checked the city's growth, the census in 1814 showing a decrease of 2,312 from 1810. In Aug. 1812, experiments with gas lights were made in the park. Fulton's steam frigate was launched in Oct. 1814. In 1821 the survey and laying out of the island north of Houston street was completed after 10 years' labor. In the winter of this year the Hudson river was frozen over for the first time in 41 years. Yellow fever reappeared in 1822, occasioning a great panic; the city south of the park was fenced off and nearly deserted, families, merchants, banks, and even the city government removing to Greenwich (now the 9th ward) and upper Broadway; yet the mortality was not comparatively great, fewer than 200 persons being victims. This panic materially improved property north of Canal street, and correspondingly expanded the city. In 1823 interments south of Canal street were forbidden, Washington square was regulated, and a gas company was organized—gas being first generally used two years later. The city now had 12 wards, and was growing at the rate of 1,000 to 1,500 houses per year—a growth occasioned by the completion of the Erie canal, the first boat from which arrived Nov. 4, 1825. The canal celebration was the grandest affair ever known in the country. In the next decade New York received some severe blows from pestilence, fire, and financial disaster. The cholera appeared in 1832, carrying off 3,513 persons, and again in 1834, taking 971. On Dec. 16, 1835, the most disastrous fire known to the city swept the 1st ward east of Broadway and below Wall street, destroying 648 of the most valuable stores, the merchants' exchange and the South Dutch church, and property valued at more than $18,000,000. With almost miraculous energy the city was rising from these ashes, when the financial explosion of 1837 came, with suspension of specie payments, failures, and bankruptcy throughout the country. Even this, however, but momentarily checked the progress of the city, her population increasing from 202,600 in 1830 to 312,700 in 1840. In 1842 the Croton water was introduced. On July 19, 1845, a great fire occurred between Broadway, Exchange place, Broad and Stone streets, destroying over $5,000,000 worth of property. Within 40 years theatres have been burned as follows: the Park in 1821 and 1848; the Bowery in 1828, 1836, 1838 and 1845; the Mount Pitt circus in 1828; La Fayette in 1829; the National in 1839 and 1841; Niblo's in 1846; the Franklin in 1849. In 1849, by legislative act and vote of the people, radical changes were made in the city charter, the selection of leading officers being opened to popular suffrage, and the police partially (since wholly) taken from the control of the mayor. The most serious popular disturbance of recent times was the Astor place riot in May, 1849, growing out of the assumed hostility of two prominent actors. Cholera came again in the summer of 1849 and carried off 5,071 persons; and lastly in 1854, when 374 died. The first city railroad was built in 1852, in anticipation of the projected industrial exhibition, which opened with great ceremony (the president of the United States officiating) July 14, 1853, in a magnificent crystal palace in the form of a Greek cross, built of iron and glass, 365½ feet in diameter each way, with galleries, and a dome 123 feet high and 100 wide, the flooring covering 5¾ acres. This building was burned in 1858. In 1857 occurred another financial panic, but its consequences were not extensively disastrous. In the same year the radical change in the control of the police made by the legislature, and the resistance to the act by Mayor Wood, resulted in popular disturbances in June and July. The first serious trouble was on June 9, when a conflict occurred for the possession of the street commissioner's office—the governor having appointed a new head, and the mayor refusing to deliver the keys. An order was issued for the arrest of the mayor, and a detachment of the new or metropolitan police went with the officer to serve it. They were resisted by the old or municipal police, who adhered to the mayor, and a savage fight ensued on the steps of the city hall; many were hurt, but none killed. The 7th regiment chanced to be on parade for a visit to Boston, and were summoned to the city hall. The governor of the state came to the city, but the whole matter was soon transferred to the courts in the form of a suit for possession of the disputed office. There was no further disturbance until July 3, when the decision of the court of appeals sustaining the new police law was announced. This law had been violently denounced by the mayor, and the more turbulent and dangerous of the people openly resisted it. Under pretence of obedience to the court of last resort, the mayor disbanded his police on the eve of the national celebration. On the 4th the usual license of a holiday led to various disturbances, resulting finally in a serious conflict known as the 'dead rabbit riot.' The dead rabbits were a faction of the rowdy and vagabond boys and young men of the Five Points, mostly composed of thieves and convicts. On the night of the 3d they attacked the police patrolmen in the Bowery, but were driven off by another faction known as Bowery boys. The next day an assault was made upon the police in Jackson street, and in the evening there was a series of fights in the Five Points, where even the women threw bricks, stones, pots and kettles at the police from the tops of the houses. The Bowery boys mingled in the fight also, and for hours there was a running contest over most of the 6th ward. There was some pistol firing, and the mob got possession of a howitzer, but did not use it. Order was restored by calling out a detachment of the military, who marched to and fro over the ground, where they found piles of bricks and stones, ready for use by the mob. Some of the police were badly bruised, and one died from his wounds; 11 persons in all lost their lives through this riot.—The original charter of New York city was granted by James II. in 1686, amended by Queen Anne in 1708, further enlarged by George II. in 1730, confirmed by the general assembly of the province in 1732, and specially affirmed after the revolution by the state legislature. This charter was of the most liberal nature; it made New York practically a free government, established an elective council, and gave unusual privileges to the people. The most important property grants were the exclusive possession and control of the waters to low water mark on all the shores opposite Manhattan island, with the ownership of the ferries for all time, and the proprietorship of all waste and unoccupied lands on the island. The 'mayor, aldermen, and commonalty' were made a perpetual corporation; municipal officers were created; an annual election was ordered, at which all freeholders and those made freemen by act of the city might vote; full power was conferred to make roads, bridges, and ferries, establish markets, regulate the sale of merchandise, make free citizens, hold courts and administer justice, erect and own wharfs, grant licenses for all manner of retail trade, and to all necessary acts for the establishment and maintenance of the government. The mayor was appointed by the provincial governor and council until the revolution; by the state governor and council of appointment until 1821; by the common council until 1834; and thenceforward by the people in general election. No direct changes were made in this charter for 100 years; but much of the judicial power had been transferred to regular courts, and the number of members of the common council had increased with the growth of the city. In 1829 the people in city convention prepared, and the legislature adopted, the amended charter of 1830. It divided the common council into two boards of concurrent powers, gave the mayor a veto, and provided against extravagance by prohibiting the drawing of money from the treasury except upon previous specific appropriations. The next amendments were made in 1849, when the government was divided into 7 departments, the head of each being elected by the people; the mayor's term was extended to two years; and further checks were put upon hasty or wasteful expenditures by requiring previous publicity and prohibiting members of the common council from being interested in city work. In 1853 the board of assistant aldermen was changed to a board of 60 councilmen, the term of aldermen extended to two years, and city works and property were ordered to be let or sold by contract or at auction; the aldermen were displaced from the court of sessions and the oyer and terminer, and the appointment of policemen (up to this time made practically by the aldermen) was confided to the mayor, city judge, and recorder. The last and most important changes were made by the amendments of 1857; the city was redistricted for aldermen, reducing the number from 22 to 17; the 60 councilmen were reduced to 24; the aldermen were no longer supervisors, a new county board being created; the mayor and common council were entirely dissevered from the police; the salaries of aldermen and councilmen were abolished (but have since been restored), and their powers were materially restricted, particularly in the license for selling liquors, that duty going to a special commission; the mode of choosing heads of departments was changed in several instances from election to appointment by the mayor and aldermen; some departments were abolished; and still further safeguards were enacted against reckless expense, by requiring a nearly unanimous vote to exceed certain specified appropriations, and making malfeasance on the part of a member of the common council an indictable offense. But with all these changes, the charter of 1730, known as the 'Montgomerie charter,' is recognised as the fountain head of city government, and upon its liberal provisions rest the vast public, and private interests of the municipality."

In 1860, Abraham Lincoln, the Republican candidate, was elected President of the United States. The result of this election so exasperated the South, believing, as they did, that it was a declaration of determined hostility on the part of the North, that they began at once to demand secession, and it was but a few weeks before eleven of the States seceded from the Union. In the attempt by the Government to provision Fort Sumter, April, 1861, the first gun was fired by the Confederate troops, assembled at Charleston, and the rebellion was fully inaugurated. The excitement in the city of New York, when the telegraph brought the news of the firing upon Fort Sumter, was intense. Immediately the city prepared for war. Money was freely voted, and troops sent forward; barracks were thrown up on all the public squares, and Broadway formed a portion of the highway for all the northern and eastern troops on their way to Washington. Business of every kind, except that which was connected with furnishing supplies to the Government, was paralysed. Fortunes were rapidly lost in one direction and made in the other. In July, 1863, the great riot occurred—resistance to the draft being the nominal occasion, though many believed it to be fomented by Southern emissaries, especially as its greatest fury was mainly directed against the negroes. For a few days the city seemed to be given up to the demon of misrule, owing to the inefficiency of the rulers, and people were murdered, houses were pillaged and burned, and property to a very large amount destroyed, but it was finally arrested, as such riots only can be, by a free discharge of grape shot; the most merciful and effective remedy for such a disease.

In November, 1864, Mr. Lincoln was re-elected President by a very large vote, and in the spring of 1865, he was assassinated in the theatre at Washington, by John Wilkes Booth. The whole country was stunned at the news, and in the city of New York the hearts of men, women and children, were bowed in grief. The day of the funeral ceremonies will be remembered by every one who witnessed them. Every house, every church, and in fact, every building and every street in the city, was draped in black. A month or two later the war was brought to a close; and Broadway was again the marching ground for the soldiers; but now, it was for home they were bound. They were welcomed with salvos of artillery, and what was better, with plentifully supplied tables; the barracks disappeared, and the city again assumed its normal air. The total number of troops furnished to the war by the city was 116,382.

In 1866 the city was threatened with another visitation of cholera, but nothing serious came of it. In May of this year the Academy of Music was burned.

In 1870, a new charter for the city was passed by the legislature. Under it, the Mayor and Common Council, (consisting of Aldermen and Assistant Aldermen,) are elected by the people at large, the Aldermen being chosen on a general ticket. The Street and Aqueduct Departments are consolidated in one, called the Department of Public Works, and a Department of Docks, Department of Public Parks, a Fire Department, a Health Department, and a Police Board are created, the heads of which are all appointed by the Mayor. The old Board of Supervisors was abolished by another bill. This charter took effect in May, 1870. The year 1871 will be memorable to the city on account of the great riot occasioned by the parade of the Orangemen, July 12, which was only suppressed after the loss of a number of lives; and also for the fearful destruction of human life by the explosion of the Staten Island Ferry steamer, Westfield, on Sunday, July 30—by which more than a hundred people were killed, and a large number wounded.

§ 3. Sanitary Provisions.

Strangers will be interested in knowing what public provisions are made here for the safety and comfort, not only of the inhabitants of the city, but also, what security against accident there may be, and what treatment they are likely to receive themselves in case of any accident or of sudden illness. From the first report of the newly-organized Board of Health, and from the Report of the Superintendent of Buildings, therefore, we make the following extracts, which will go to show that security against accident and the care of the public health are in the hands of intelligent and faithful officers, and that, to secure this end, all known means are provided; such as security against unsafe buildings; fire-escapes; the ambulance system, for saving life and lessening suffering; and public urinals and drinking hydrants:

UNSAFE BUILDINGS.—" 1,073 buildings reported to be unsafe have been examined, and of these, 61 have been taken down and entirely removed, 730 have been made safe and secure—the balance being either in process of removal or being made secure."

FIRE-ESCAPES.—"2,678 fire-escapes have been provided for buildings reported as requiring means of escape in case of fire, during the year ending April 5th, 1871. During the year several instances have occurred, where life would, undoubtedly, have been sacrificed but for the means of escape thus provided.

"In regard to hotels, proceedings have been instituted to render them more secure in this respect—and, with a single exception, all the owners and proprietors of these buildings have expressed their willingness to co-operate with the Department as soon as proper plans can be adopted which will insure safety. On some of the hotels, these improvements are already in progress."

THE AMBULANCE SYSTEM.—The ambulance system, established in 1869, has been found of inestimable value as a means of saving life and reducing suffering. Six ambulances have been provided, and, under the rules established, horses stand harnessed day and night, ready to be attached for the conveyance of persons wounded or taken ill in the public streets. The ambulances are equipped with surgical instruments, bandages, restoratives, etc.; and, on notice by telegraph from a police station of the occurrence of a casualty, an ambulance is dispatched in charge of a surgeon, who applies such remedies as may be required, and determines, from the condition of the patient, whether he may be safely removed to his home, or to Bellevue, or the Reception Hospital. During the past year there have been 1,401 patients thus removed; of whom, 1,066 were received from the several police precinct stations, 297 transferred from the Reception Hospital to Bellevue Hospital, and 38 from private residences. By the demolition of the New York Hospital, the city was deprived of hospital accommodation below Twenty-sixth street. The area south of that street comprises six square miles, and contains a resident population of 300,000 persons; but, throughout the business hours of the day, it may safely be assumed, the population gathered from all parts of the city and the adjacent country is at least three-fold, or, nearly 1,000,000—besides containing three-fourths of the shipping of the port. In that crowded and busy portion of the city, the larger number of casualties occur. To atone for the great public loss by the destruction of the New York Hospital, the Legislature of 1868 directed the Commissioners to provide a Reception Hospital at some point south of Grand street; but, because of an error in the language of the act, the law was inoperative. The Legislature, at the last session, corrected the error; and the Commissioners endeavored, though unsuccessfully, to find a suitable site, till the Commissioners of the Public Parks generously assigned them the temporary use of a building in the City Hall Park. The urgent need of reception hospitals has been demonstrated during the past summer. Since the 27th of June last to the 1st of January, there have been received at the Reception Hospital in the Park, 723 patients who had been wounded or taken seriously ill in the streets. Of this number, according to the testimony of the physician in charge, 72 patients would have died in the ambulance, had the attempt been made to convey them to Bellevue Hospital or to their homes.

§ 3. Population of the City, Present and Past.

Full returns of the census of 1870 give a grand total of 942,292, as the population of this municipality; of this number, 510,553 are native whites, 418,646 are whites of foreign birth, and 13,093 are colored.

The following table shows the increase in the number of inhabitants since 1790:

Years.	Population.	Years.	Population.
1790	23,133	1840	312,710
1800	60,529	1850	512,547
1810	96,373	1860	813,662
1820	123,706	1870	942,292
1830	197,091		

CHAPTER III.

IMPORTANT IMPROVEMENTS IN PROGRESS.

1. Improvement in Docks and Piers.—2. The Viaduct Railway.—3. The Brooklyn Bridge.—4. The Great Union Passenger Railroad Depot.

§ 1. Improvement in Docks.

When the present Commission of the Department of Docks was organized by the Legislature, they found the property committed to their care utterly inadequate to accommodate the immense commerce of the port, all the existing wharves, piers, and bulkheads being built of perishable materials, in a very imperfect manner; the piers being too narrow to allow vessels to load or discharge cargo at both sides thereof simultaneously, and of insufficient length to afford accommodations for large steamers engaged in the European trade. In consequence of this want of accommodation, several lines of steamers now occupy wharves in New Jersey, which doubtless would have come to New York had the proper provision been made for them here.

The greater number of existing piers and bulkheads were found to require extensive repairs, and many of them to be wholly or partially rebuilt, their condition being such as to render them totally unfit for commercial purposes.

After advertising for plans for improvements, and maturely considering all that have been laid before them, the following is, in brief, the plan they propose:

First. To construct a permanent river wall of Béton and masonry, or masonry alone, so far outside of the existing bulkheads as to give a river street 250 feet wide along the North River, 200 feet wide on the East River, from the Battery to Thirty-first Street, and 175 feet wide north of that point.

Second. To build piers projecting from the river wall, of ample dimensions, adequate construction, and, so far as possible, affording an unobstructed passage for the water.

Third. Whenever it is necessary, to cover these piers with substantial sheds suitable to the requirements of each case.

In carrying into execution the proposed improvements along the water front of New York, it is obvious that they should be extended only as the requirements of commerce demand.

The commerce of New York is now accommodated by the following extent of wharf facilities, viz:

North River, from the Battery to Sixty-first Street, a bulkhead with an aggregate length of 23,163 feet, and an aggregate length of piers of 31,229 feet, with a pier area of 1,606,024 square feet.

East River, from the Battery to Fifty-first Street, 26,494 feet of bulkhead, and an aggregate length of piers of 19,139 feet, with a pier area of 716,644 square feet.

Thus the bulkhead and piers together give a wharf line of 150,293 feet, or 28½ miles, with a pier area of 2,322,668 square feet. By wharf line is meant all that portion of the river wall and piers that vessels can approach. Considerable portions of this wharf line are practically useless from insufficient depth of water and other causes. The proposed arrangement of the water front, including the new river wall, and a far better disposition of the piers, gives, on the North River, from the Battery to Sixty-first Street, a river wall line of 25,743 feet, and a pier length of 37,529 feet, with a pier area of 3,325,600 square feet; and on the East River, from the Battery to Fifty-first Street, a river wall line of 27,995 feet, and a pier length of about 28,000 feet, with a pier area of about 1,780,009 square feet.

Thus in the proposed system the piers and river wall together will give a wharf line of about 195,000 feet, or about 37 miles, and the piers alone will have an area of about 5,105,000 square feet, sufficient, it is safe to say, to accommodate a commerce vastly greater than that which now finds its way to the water front of New York.

The proposed arrangement will give, between Grand

Street and West Eleventh Street, a wharf line of 21 43-100 miles (greater than the whole existing quay line of Liverpool, including the new constructions at Birkenhead, which amount in all to about 20¾ miles), against an existing line within the same limits of 20 7-100 miles, and from the superiority of the arrangement in the increased width of the piers, slips, and river streets, and the greater depth of water making every foot available for use, will accommodate with ease a much greater commerce than now exists.

§ 2. The Viaduct Railway.

The Act of the Legislature authorizing this Company is as follows:

"The Company is authorized to construct two Viaduct Railways or branches through the city of New York, on the east and west sides thereof, from a common starting point at or near Chambers street, between Broadway and Chatham street: also across the Harlem River and through Westchester County: with power to build additional lines of railway or branches, from time to time, in any part of the City or Westchester County. *The property acquired by the Company is exempted from taxes and assessments during the period allowed for the final completion of the railway in the city.* The Mayor, Aldermen, and Commonalty of New York are authorized and directed with the approval of the Commissioners of the Sinking Fund, to subscribe for Five Millions of dollars of the stock of the Company, whenever one million of dollars thereof has been subscribed for by private parties. [*This conditional amount of stock has been wholly subscribed for and taken by the Directors of the Company.*] On the completion of either of the lines of railway to the line of Westchester County, the Supervisors of that County are authorized to issue the bonds of the County to such amount as the Supervisors shall deem expedient, to aid in the construction and extension of the railway in and through that County. For the proper equalization of the interest of shareholders who may subscribe, and pay in moneys at different times, the Directors are authorized to issue scrip for interest on such payments, payable out of the earnings."

The want of some means of rapid transit between the lower, business portion of the city, and the upper end of the Island and Westchester County, has already driven hundreds of thousands of New Yorkers to seek domicils across the rivers, on Long Island and in New Jersey. Various plans to accomplish this transit have been proposed, discussed, and abandoned as impracticable, until at last, the Viaduct Railway has been projected, approved, authorized, and the execution of the project is committed to some of the wealthiest and most prominent men in the city, who are so sanguine of its feasibility and completion that it is already looked upon as an accomplished fact.

§ 3. The Brooklyn Bridge.

This long-needed means of additional facilities of communication with its principal suburb, is now in a fair way of being realized by the City of New York. The new bridge will be of more importance perhaps to Brooklyn than to New York, if we regard them as distinct cities; but, in fact, Brooklyn is as much a part of New York as Harlem is. More than 100,000 of its male inhabitants cross over the ferries to New York every day to their business; their bedrooms and their business being much nearer together than they would be if they lived above Twentieth street, in New York City. The day is probably not far distant when the two cities will be incorporated under one government.

The work on the bridge is progressing rapidly. The abutment on the Brooklyn side already towers above the surrounding objects, and the work of dredging is going on on the New York side, preparatory to laying the caisson. The landing place on the New York side will be near that of the Viaduct Railway, in the vicinity of the City Hall Park. The Brooklyn terminus it is expected will be somewhere in the vicinity of the corner of Sands and Fulton streets. But, it will take several years to complete the work.

§ 4. The Union Railroad Passenger Depot.

The Great Union Railroad Passenger Depot at Forty-second street is at length completed; and the passenger trains of the New York and New Haven, the Harlem and the Hudson River Railroads are all now accommodated with a depot under one roof.

This magnificent structure, the largest of its kind, and incomparably the most elegant in the country, the most complete, and the best adapted for its purposes of any in the world, is a noble and fit monument to the foresight of its eminent projector, and is well worth a visit and careful inspection by any stranger.

The building extends from Forty-second street to Forty-fifth street, 692 feet; and, from Fourth avenue to a new street on the west side, which runs from Forty-second to Forty-fifth street, 240 feet, and has an average height of 60 feet. On three sides the walls are of brick, with iron trimmings. The Forty-fifth street front is cast-iron. The roof is wrought-iron, supported by semi-circular trusses 199 feet span, and has a clear height of 90 feet, covered with galvanized iron and glass. The building is in the Renaissance style of architecture, and is supplied with every necessary appointment.

The basement story is occupied by two large restaurants for gentlemen, and two for ladies and gentlemen; and has five large stores for general business purposes. The ground floor on the Forty-second street front is occupied by the New Haven Company for waiting and baggage-rooms; the side on the new street by the Harlem and Hudson River Companies for the same purposes; the trains entering at the Forty-fifth street front. The second story furnishes business offices for the three companies.

The car-house has capacity to contain 150 passenger-cars. Passengers for the trains are admitted by way of the waiting-rooms. City horse-cars will be admitted to the depot on the arrival of trains, for the accommodation of passengers. In each waiting-room is a telegraph office and a newspaper stand.

CHAPTER IV.

PUBLIC PARKS AND SQUARES.

1. The Central Park.—2. The Battery.—3. The Bowling Green.—4. The City Hall Park.—5. Washington Square.—6. Tompkins Square.—7. Union Square.—8. Madison Square.—9. Mount Morris Square.

§ 1. The Central Park.

[One of the departments organized under the new charter of the city, is the *Department of Public Parks*. The commissioners appointed under this act have charge of all the parks, squares, and boulevards of the city; and, under their administration, a vigorous and radical improvement has been, or is now, making in every park or square in the city.]

If that object be entitled to be called the most attractive which has the most visitors, Central Park may be fairly pronounced New York City's chiefest attraction.

It is centrally located on the island; being bounded by 59th street on the south and 110th street on the north, by the 5th avenue on the east and the 8th avenue on the west. In form, it is an elongated parallelogram —about two and a half miles in length, and half a mile in width. The southern boundary of the park is about the same distance from the Battery, as the northern is from the extreme northern point of the island; to wit, about five and a half miles.

ACCESS.—The Park is readily accessible from every portion of the city; having several gates of entrance at each end, as well as along its sides.

The *Eighth ave.* street cars will drop visitors at the south-west corner of the Park, which is an entrance for pedestrians, equestrians, or carriages. These cars also stop at all the entrances on the west side of the Park above this entrance. The *Sixth ave.* street cars run to the 59th street gate, which is an entrance for pedestrians and equestrians.

The *Broadway* street cars will drop passengers at the 7th ave. gate, which is for pedestrians only. The *Belt*

Line street-cars drop visitors at either of these 59th street gates.

The principal carriage entrance is at 59th street and Fifth ave.; the entrance gates on this avenue are most easily reached from the *Third ave.* street cars. The gates are at 72d, 79th, 90th, 96th, 102d, and 110th streets; the last is the carriage entrance from the northeast.

The fare on all these street cars to 59th street is five cents; on the Eighth ave. line, above 59th street, to 72d street, 8 cents; above that, 10 cents; and on Third ave. line above 65th street, 1 cent.

Having landed at either of these entrances, the visitor has three different ways before him to see the Park. He may, if a good walker and have the time, see it best on foot. If he would ride, and at the same time study economy, he may get into one of the Park carriages, which will be found at the south-west corner of the Park at Eighth ave., and, for 25 cents, he will be carried the whole circuit of the Park to the starting place. We would recommend him, however, to be let out of the carriage on the west side of the Ramble, which he may then visit; after which, he can go to the Terrace by way of the Lake, and then on by way of the Mall to any one of the 59th street gates. This would, however, give but a limited idea of the things to be seen in the Park, as he will readily discover, if he will buy a Park guide (Miller's is probably the best), before he goes there. The third plan is, to take a carriage from your hotel, or hire one at some of the gates, when as much time may be given to the excursion as the visitor pleases —but, bear in mind that, to see many of the most interesting things in the Park, one must spend a great deal of time on his feet.

The total area of the Park is	. .	862 acres
Length of carriage drives, completed	. .	9½ miles
" bridle roads "	. .	5¼ "
" walks "	. .	28 "

The most interesting portion of the Park to many visitors will be the *Ramble*, which can only be seen while on foot. Then, there are the *Terrace*, the *Mall*, the *Central Lake*, the *Museum*, the *Zoological Garden*, the *Reservoirs*, the *Belvedere*, the *Bridges*, etc., etc.; all objects of interest. The skating season, which begins about Christmas, but is of uncertain duration, is a favorite time for many people to visit the Park. Visitors must bear in mind that the scene changes every month—that the flowers and foliage of June give place to those of later dates; and, if they would see all there is to be seen in the Park, they must visit it frequently and at different seasons of the year.

The plan of our Guide-Book does not admit of a description of the various interesting objects to be seen in the Park. To point out and describe them would require a volume larger than we propose to make. Our task is done when we give the location, means of access, and advise how best to see it.

The Proposed Art Museum in Central Park.—By a recent act of the Legislature of the State, which has received the approval of the Governor, the Board of Commissioners of Public Parks are authorized to erect and maintain upon that portion of Central Park known as Manhattan Square, a suitable building for the use of the Metropolitan Museum of Art. The same act also authorizes the city authorities to issue bonds to the amount of a million of dollars, the proceeds of which are to be appropriated to the erection of two buildings—one for the Museum of Art, the other for the Museum of Natural History. Already a large sum has been subscribed by our wealthy citizens for the purchase of pictures, and negotiations are proceeding for the acquisition of a valuable collection of European pictures. Works of art of all kinds will be provided for; coins, vases, bronzes, manuscripts, etc., etc.; and it is the intention of the trustees, among whom are some of our most public-spirited citizens, to establish an institution that shall take rank among the first in the world.

§ 2. The Battery.

The old New Yorker who remembers the Battery fifty years ago; when around it were congregated the most fashionable residences and the wealthiest people of the city; when it was the great fashionable promenade and flirting ground of the city; will scarcely believe now, that there is any longer such a place. Fashion deserted it years ago, and the once elegant residences of the city's nabobs are now turned into stores, and emigrant boarding-houses. Castle Garden has become the emigrant landing place, and the Battery a sad reminiscence of better days. But the Battery, in its natural advantages, has attractions as a place of recreation, unsurpassed, probably, by those of any similar public place in the world. The magnificent view of the harbor, always alive with the movement of ships and steamers and the scenery of its surrounding shores, the fresh invigorating sea breeze combine to make it at once the most wholesome and the most inspiriting means of bodily and mental refreshment within the immediate reach of our citizens. The Battery, with the improvements which have been put upon it, has been rendered a delightful place for the wearied toilers in its vicinity, and an attractive resort for the stranger. The sea wall has been completed, and a large space filled in; the grounds laid out in plots, elegant and picturesque in appearance, and over a thousand trees and bushes have been planted. When the stranger is on the Battery, let him not forget to look at the house at the S. W. corner of Broadway and State street, called now the Washington Hotel. This, in Revolutionary times, was the *Kennedy House*, where Washington and Lee had their head-quarters, and is one of the very few houses left in the city which can date so far back as the days of the Revolution.

§ 3. The Bowling Green.

This spot has always been a prominent point of interest to the New Yorker as well as to the stranger visitor. Here, in 1780, was erected an Equestrian statue of

George III., made of lead ; a few years later, soldiers and citizens joined in pulling it down, and the lead was run into bullets which were used by the soldiers in the American army. Several attempts at improving this spot have been made within the last half century. A few New Yorkers will remember the first fountain erected there—denounced by some as an unsightly pile of stones—and the two beautiful flamingoes which were kept there. The railing around the Green, a relic of Revolutionary times, has been repaired and painted, and the gates and coping reset. The fountain has been put in good order, and is kept playing, the ground sodded, new walks laid out, with posts and chains guarding them, and neat settees provided for the comfort of wayfarers, and of those who may desire to frequent this conveniently situated little spot. New trees have been substituted for those which were dead or dying, and shrubbery, and flowers added, and it has been made one of the most beautiful and attractive places in the city.

§ 4. The City Hall Park

Is becoming so encumbered with buildings that it requires some stretch of the imagination to call it a park. The city hall, new court-house, old court-houses and record office we have already become familiar with, and now comes the new post-office, which appropriates a large slice of the southern end of the park. But with all these drawbacks the City Hall Park will always be an attractive point in the city. The new commissioners have vastly improved this park during the past year in every respect. They have added to the width of the carriage-way in Broadway, the space formerly used for walks; removed the old iron railing, repaired all the sidewalks with the improved asphaltun pavement, and the present condition of the City Hall Park, with its cultivated enclosures, its trees, shrubbery, fountains and paved walks, commands universal approval.

§ 5. **Washington Square**.

[Bounded by Macdougal street on the west, Waverley Place on the north, University Place on the east, and Fourth street on the south.]

Washington Square has an area of about ten acres. It was used, until within forty or fifty years, as a Potter's Field. In 1832 it was converted into a park. It has long been a popular breathing-place for the section of the city in which it is situated. It is surrounded by houses which were once considered elegant, and were occupied by the wealthy and fashionable people of the city; now they are rapidly coming into use for boarding-houses; wealth and fashion having traveled farther north.

Fifth avenue has just been opened through this square, connecting with Laurens street on its south side, and the Square has undergone similar treatment at the hands of the commissioners, which the other squares and parks have been subjected to, and in consequence, its appearance is vastly improved. On the east side of the Square the visitor will notice the N. Y. University, a very elegant marble building in the Gothic style, 180 feet by 100, completed in 1836.

§ 6. **Tompkins' Square**.

[Bounded by Avenue A on the west, Tenth street on the north, Avenue B on the east, and Seventh street on the south.]

This Square is located in a thickly settled portion of the city, and is surrounded by densely occupied tenement houses. It has long been used as a parade ground by the First Division of militia, and the improvements made upon it are subordinate to this use. A new grass plot forty feet in width has been laid around the interior border, and within this a walk of twenty-five feet for promenading. On the outer side of this walk rows of deciduous trees have already been planted, interspersed with lamps and benches, and settees, in order that persons may have places of rest to enjoy the reviews of the military or the promenade afforded by the walks. Deciduous trees have also been planted all around the square; the exterior sidewalk has been covered with asphalt pavement; two large public urinals, sufficiently protected by evergreens, have been placed in the Square, and two keepers' houses. Indeed, the whole place has been made inviting.

§ 7. Union Square.

[Bounded by Broadway on the west, Seventeenth st. on the north, Fourth avenue on the east, Fourteenth st. on the south.]

The visitor will remark that all sorts of figures receive the name of squares in the city of New York, and Union Square is no exception. This *square* is an oval in shape, and is one of the prettiest parks in the city. It is, however, undergoing transformation, and will, doubtless, soon be far more attractive than it is now. The iron railing is to be removed, and the walks covered with asphalt. The statues of Washington and Lincoln are to be surrounded with handsome railings and ornamental lamps, and urns filled with flowers during the warm season, will be erected at short distances.

The statue of Washington at the south end of the square, which the visitor will not fail to remark, is the work of H. K. Brown. It is of a rich bronze, and weighs four tons, and is fourteen feet in height, standing on a pedestal of the same height, and is generally regarded as an admirable work of art. At the western angle of the square is a bronze statue of Mr. Lincoln.

§ 8. Madison Square.

[Bounded by Broadway and Fifth avenue on the west, by Twenty-Sixth street on the north, by Madison avenue on the east, and by Twenty-Third street on the south.]

Under the new regime has been completely transformed. The railing has been taken away, and it remains open on all sides like **Washington** Square and the City Hall Park. Sufficient space has been taken off the Broadway and Fifth avenue sides of the square to widen those throughfares seventy-five feet. The sidewalk surrounding the Worth monument is in the form of a small circle, and seat-room and shelter are provided for those who wish to rest there. Another small plot of ground just below the Worth monument, has been laid out and handsomely ornamented. The walks in the Square, while being so planned as to please the eye, by an apparent variety of serpentine windings, are yet so laid out as to give access in almost a straight line across the Square from the streets from one side to the other. The centre of the square is laid out as a lawn, on which there is a handsome stand for the musicians. At each end of the square there is a new and beautiful fountain. There is a "ladies' cottage" erected in the northeastern corner, and all the conveniences found in the other parks and squares, will be found here. The square will be thickly studded with the improved street lamps, like those used in Washington Square, and will be surrounded with trees.

On this square stands the monument to Gen. Worth, above alluded to, erected by the city in 1857. The monument is four-sided, each side having inscriptions with bronze reliefs in memory of the deceased. A handsome equestrian figure of the General, in high relief, with armorial insignia, may be seen on the southern side, and the names of several of the celebrated battle-fields in which the General distinguished himself; and on the other sides will be found the names of other battle-fields, date and place of the General's birth, etc.

§ 9. Mount Morris Square,

[Bounded by 124th st. on the north, Madison avenue on the east, 120th st. on the south, and by a street between Fifth and Sixth avenues on the west.]

Is the great public park of Harlem, and one of the most eligible locations on the island for capabilities of ornamentation. The roads rising far above the grades of the adjacent streets, make it an agreeable place of resort when the atmosphere is clear, and a walk up the hill is inviting. That portion of this park on the grade of the surrounding streets is already completed, and is not inferior to any other park in the city.

CHAPTER V.

PUBLIC BUILDINGS.

1. Trinity Church.—2. The Post-Office.—3. U. S. Treasury Building.—4. The Custom House.—5. The City Hall.—6. The New Court House.—7. The Cooper Institute.—8. The National Academy of Design.—9. The Y. M. C. Association Building.

§ 1. Trinity Church

Is probably the most elegant church edifice at present in the city. It stands on Broadway directly opposite Wall st., and its steeple, like the dome of St. Peter's at Rome, is the most prominent object the stranger sees as he approaches the city. The parish of Trinity church is probably the oldest, as it is certainly the wealthiest, Episcopal church in the country. "In the fifth year of the reign of William and Mary, 1697, by act of Assembly, approved and ratified by the Governor of the province, a royal grant and confirmation were made of a certain *church and the steeple*, lately built in the city of New York, together with a certain piece of ground without the N. gate of the city, commonly called and known by name of Broadway, with the parish of Trinity church."

Religious services, in the Episcopal form, had been held in the chapel within the fort many years before this date. A lively old Dutch traveler, who once attended service in the fort, thus describes the clergyman: "This Schaats then preached. He had a defect in the left eye, and used such strange gestures and language, that I think I never, in all my life, have heard anything more miserable; indeed, I can compare him with no one better than with one Do. Van Ecke, lately the minister at Armoyden, in Zeeland, more in life, conversation and gestures than in person. As it is not strange in these countries to have men as ministers who drink, we could imagine nothing else than that he had been drinking a little this morning. His text was '*Come unto me all ye,*' etc., but he was so rough that even the most godless of our sailors were astonished."*

To return to the church. It was twice enlarged, once in 1735, and again in 1737. In 1776 it was destroyed by fire, and a new edifice was completed only in 1790. In 1839 this building was taken down and the present church was begun, and completed in 1846. The material of which the church is built is New Jersey sandstone. The building is 192 feet in length by 80 feet in width; height of walls 60 feet. The style is Gothic; the spire, one of the most beautiful in the country, reaches an altitude of 284 feet. In the tower is a chime of bells. The tower and spire are open to visitors *daily* except on Sunday, and during morning and evening services, which are held in the morning from nine o'clock to half-past, and in the afternoon from three to half-past three. Fee for admission to the tower and spire 12½ cents each. Visitors ascend a spiral staircase to the height of 250 feet, and the view to be had here of the city and its surroundings is the finest one can get from any known point. No traveler who desires to see the city should leave it without ascending Trinity church steeple. In a clear day almost every object within a distance of from five to ten miles from the city, is distinguishable.

The visit to Trinity church must not conclude with only seeing the edifice and the view from the steeple. Pass into the churchyard; there are no monuments here a thousand or two years old, but there are some worth any visitor's while to look at; some which will be always venerated by Americans.

The grave of " Don't give up the Ship," Lawrence, the hero of the Chesapeake, is here, near to the main entrance. Another spot of interest will be the tomb of Alexander Hamilton, whose life was sacrificed in the duel with Aaron Burr. Still another, will be the monument erected to the memory of the Americans who died

---

* Memoirs of L. I. Hist. Soc., vol. 1. (Journal of a Voyage to N.Y. in 1679–80.) p. 112.

in the British prisons. The visitor will find many other graves which will interest him, and he can while away an hour in these grounds very profitably.

§ 2. The Post-Office.

The present Post-office is not noteworthy for its architecture, though it is for its history. It is the oldest church edifice now remaining in the city. It was formerly the Middle Dutch church, and was erected before the Revolution. Portions of its interior woodwork and its steeple were brought from Holland. At the time of the Revolution it was on the extreme northern boundary of the city. When the British took possession of the city in 1776, they occupied it for a barracks for their soldiers. Afterwards it was converted into a hospital; finally the pews were removed, and it was used for a riding school. It was again occupied as a church in 1790. It was purchased by the Government for a Post-office in 1861.

It is located in Nassau st., east side, and covers the width of the block from Liberty to Cedar sts., and is one block east from Broadway. It is open at all hours, day and night, the night window on Nassau st. being open to callers from 6.30, P. M., to 7.30, A. M. Sundays the office is open only from 9 to 11, A. M.

ENTRANCE TO APARTMENTS.

Newspaper, Registry and Money Order Departments, Nassau Street, first door from Liberty Street.

Stamp Department, Wholesale and Retail, Nassau Street, second door from Liberty Street.

Ladies' Department, Nassau Street, third door from Liberty Street.

General Delivery and Advertised Letter Department, Nassau Street, fourth door from Liberty Street.

Letter Drops for Domestic and City Mails, Nassau Street, fifth door from Liberty Street.

Box Delivery Department, Cedar Street, corner Nassau Street.

Foreign Department and Drops for Foreign Letters, Cedar Street, last door from Nassau Street.

Dead Letter Department (hours 10 to 3,) Cedar Street, Up-Stairs.

Postmaster's, Assistant Postmaster's, and Cashier's Offices (hours 10 to 3,) Cedar Street, Up-Stairs.

Carriers' Department, Cedar Street, fourth door from Nassau Street.

STATIONS OR BRANCH POST-OFFICES.

Station A is located at	-	No. 100 Spring Street.
Station B	" - -	No. 382 Grand Street.
Station C	" - -	No. 627 Hudson Street.
Station D	"	No. 12 Bible House, Astor Place.
Station E	" - -	No. 465 Eighth Avenue.
Station F	" - -	No. 342 Third Avenue.
Station G	" - -	No. 735 Seventh Avenue.
Station H	" - -	No. 978 Third Avenue.
Station K	"	Yorkville, 86th Street, near 3d Ave.
Station L	"	Harlem, 1,922 3d Ave, near 124th St.
Station M	"	Washington Heights, 10th Ave. near 158th Street.

The stations are open from 6.30 A. M. to 8 P. M., with the exception of stations "G," "H" and "K" which close at 7.30 P. M. On Sundays the Stations are open from 8 to 9.30 A. M., for the sale of postage stamps and the delivery of letters.

Strangers are recommended to have their letters addressed to the care of their bankers or merchant friends, or to the hotel where they intend to stop. In case they are going to a private house they can have their letters addressed to the street No. of the house. If properly directed they will not fail to reach them in due time, as there are several deliveries of letters a day all over the city by letter carriers.

*** It may not be out of place here to caution people *never to send money in a letter*—send money order or check, payable to order.

The Government is now erecting a splendid building on the south end of the City Hall Park for a new Post-office, which will be an architectural ornament to the city, and sufficiently spacious to accommodate the largely increasing business of the Department.

§ 3. U. S. Treasury Building

Stands on the corner of Wall st. and Nassau, extending through to Pine st., and was built for the Custom House. It occupies the site where the old Federal Hall originally stood, in the open gallery of which Gen. Washington was inaugurated first President of the United States.

The material of which this edifice is built is white marble, and the style of architecture is purely Doric, and is in imitation of the Pantheon at Athens. The building is in the form of a paralellogram, 200 feet long, and 90 feet wide; its height 80 feet. On Wall street is a portico with eight Doric columns 32 feet high and five feet ten inches in diameter, which is reached by a flight of eighteen granite steps. The rotunda is 60 feet in diameter, and is lighted from the dome which is supported by sixteen Corinthian columns, adorned with caps of exquisite workmanship. The roof is of granite. It may be seen from 10 A. M. to 3 P. M.

§ 4. The Custom House.

The building now used for the Custom House was built for the Merchants' Exchange, and occupies the entire block between Wall, William, and Hanover streets and Exchange Place. It is built of Quincy granite, and is fire proof. It is 200x171 feet, 77 feet to the cornice, and 125 to the top of the dome. In the portico which fronts on Wall street are 18 columns, 38 feet high, and 4 in diameter at their base. Each of the columns weighs nearly 45 tons. The rotunda is the principal room, and is in the centre of the building. Its diameter is 80 feet, and its height is the same. It is surmounted by a dome in which there is a large skylight rising from the centre, and resting on 8 fluted Corinthian columns of Italian marble, 41 feet high, and 5 feet in diameter. It is open to visitors from 10 A. M. to 3 P. M.

§ 5. The City Hall.

Stands nearly in the centre of the City Hall Park, facing the south. The front and the ends of the building are of white marble, the rear is of brown free-stone. The building is 216 feet long, 105 wide, and 65 high, Its style is a combination of three different orders of architecture: the Ionic, Corinthian and Composite. The building is crowned with a cupola which overlooks a large portion of the city. On the top of this cupola is a figure of justice, directly under which is a four dial clock, which is illuminated at night.

The Mayor's office is in the S. W. corner of this hall, the Chambers of the Board of Aldermen, Councilmen, and other public offices occupying the rest of the building. The Governor's Room as it is called, will be a place of interest to many strangers, from the fact that it contains portraits of many distinguished statesmen and other public functionaries—of greater or less merit—and a desk on which Washington wrote his first message to Congress. The chairs used in the first Congress are in the Aldermanic Chamber, and the chair used by Washington when he was inaugurated first President of the United States is in the Mayor's office.

§ 6. The New Court House.

In the rear of the City Hall and fronting Chambers street stands the New Court House, now in course of erection, although so far completed as to be already in part occupied. It is the most expensive and altogether the most pretentious public building the city can boast. It is built of marble, with iron beams and supports, iron staircases, iron doors (outside), and black walnut doors (inside); the floors of the halls are tiled with marble, laid on iron beams, covered with concrete. The order of architecture is mainly Corinthian. The length of the building 250 feet, and the width 150 feet: the height to the top of the pediment is 97 feet, to the top of the dome when erected will be 225 feet. The dome when finished will resemble that of the Capitol at

Washington. The portico on the front of the building on Chambers street will merit careful examination, as it is probably the best specimen of the kind of work in the country.

§ 7. The Cooper Institute

Is a large brown stone building, situated at the junction of Third and Fourth avenues, and occupies the entire block between those avenues, and Seventh and Eighth streets. It was erected by Mr. Peter Cooper, a merchant of this city, and devoted by him " to the moral, intellectual and physical improvement of his fellow-citizens, and dedicated to science and art." In the basement of the building is one of the largest public halls in the city, and the first and second stories are occupied for stores and offices, the rents from which, it is supposed, will be sufficient to meet the current expenses of the Institute. The third and upper stories are occupied for the Union or Institute. The third story is appropriated to an exhibition room, 125 feet long by 82 feet wide. In the fourth story is a series of galleries with alcoves for works of art. In the fifth story are lecture-rooms, and the library, which, with the reading-room attached, is entirely free, and has a very large number of regular readers. There is a *School of Design* for women in this Institute, and a school for instructing women in telegraphing, both of which are doing great good in the community.

§ 8. The National Academy of Design

Is on the N. W. corner of Twenty-Third street and Fourth avenue. It is a building which would attract the attention of the visitor were he to meet with it in any part of the world. The design of its exterior is said to be copied from an old Venetian palace, and is the only specimen of the style in the country. The building extends about 100 feet on Fourth avenue and 80 feet on Twenty-Third street. The main entrance is on Twenty-Third street. It is on a level with the second story, and is reached by a double flight of steps, which, by the skillful manipulation of the architect, have been made an ornament to the building. On entering, the visitor finds himself in a spacious hall, extending almost the whole length of the building. From this hall, the grand staircase leading to the exhibition-rooms will be noticed as one of the most prominent features of the building. The third story, which is lighted from the roof, is entirely devoted to exhibition-rooms. The wood-work used in the interior of the building is the various hard woods oiled and polished to show the natural grain and color of the woods. The pavement of the vestibule at the main entrance is of variegated marbles, and the floor of the great hall is laid in walnut and maple. The lower story walls are gray marble, with intervening courses of North River blue-stone; the entire elevation being thus variegated.

The regular exhibitions of the academy are, 1. *The Spring Exhibition*, which opens in April and closes about July 4. At this exhibition no pictures are admitted which have been exhibited here before. Another exhibition is held from July to November; and still another from November to March. Admission 25 cents. Season tickets one dollar. Catalogue 25 cents.

§ 9. The Y. M. C. Association Building

Is on the S. W. corner of Fourth avenue and Twenty-Third street. It is quite an imposing edifice, and is a fine specimen of the *Renaissance* order of architecture. The first floor is occupied by stores; the second and third for the purposes of the Young Men's Christian Association; a lecture-room, library, and reading-rooms, and the floor above these, for artists' studios. Strangers, especially young men, who may be staying in that part of the city, will find attractions in these rooms which render them an agreeable place in which to spend an evening.

CHAPTER VI.

PUBLIC WORKS.

. The Croton Aqueduct.—2. The High Bridge.—3. The Old Receiving Reservoir.—4. The New Receiving Reservoir.—5. The Distributing Reservoir.

§ 1. The Croton Aqueduct.

The Croton Aqueduct was designed to supply the city of New York with an abundance of pure and wholesome water. It commences about six miles above the mouth of the Croton river, where a dam has been constructed to elevate the water of the river forty feet, to the level of the head of the aqueduct, or one hundred and sixty-six feet above mean tide. The course of the aqueduct passes along the valley of the Croton to near its mouth, and thence into the valley of the Hudson. At eight miles from the Croton dam it reaches the village of Sing Sing and continues south through the villages of Tarrytown, Dobbs' Ferry, Hastings, and Yonkers.

At the latter place it leaves the bank of the Hudson, crosses the valley of Sawmill river and Tibbits' brook, thence along the side of the ridge that bounds the southerly side of Tibbits' brook valley, to within three and a half miles of the Harlem river, where the high grounds of the Hudson fall away so much as to require the aqueduct to occupy the summit of the country lying between the Hudson and East rivers.

This formation of country continues to and is terminated by the Harlem river, at the point where the aqueduct intersects it, which is one mile north-westerly from McComb's dam.

The length of the aqueduct, from the Croton dam to Harlem river, is 32.88 miles, for which distance it is an uninterrupted conduit of hydraulic stone and brick masonry. The high ground that bounds the northerly side of the Harlem river valley is very near the level of the aqueduct at that place, and the width of the valley at the aqueduct leve is about 1,450 feet, or a little over one quarter of a mile, over which the High Bridge is built, at an elevation of 114 feet above the level of high tide in the Harlem river, on which iron pipes are laid to convey the water across the valley.

The shore on the southerly side of the river is a bold, precipitous rock, rising at an angle of about 30 degrees, to a height of 220 feet, or about 100 feet above the level of the bottom of the aqueduct.

After crossing this valley, the aqueduct of masonry is resumed, and continued 2.015 miles, to the termination of the high ground on the north side of Manhattan valley.

This valley is .792 mile wide at the level of the aqueduct, below which it descends 102 feet. The conduit of masonry here gives place to iron pipes, which descend into the bottom of the valley, and rise again to the proper level on the opposite side; from which point the masonry conduit is again resumed, and crossing the asylum ridge and Clendinning valley, is continued 2.173 miles, to the receiving reservoir at York hill, now embraced within the Central Park.

In 1835 ground was first broken and the work of building this magnificent aqueduct was begun. It was completed in 1842, and cost over $12,000,000. Besides supplying the city proper, Blackwell's Island is also supplied from this source. At the present time 85,000,000 gallons of water are delivered into the city by the aqueduct every day, which is about 85 gallons to each inhabitant.

§ 2. The High Bridge.

This is a work every visitor to the city should find time to see. It may be reached by different routes. The pleasantest but most expensive will be by private carriage by way of Central Park (route described in chapter on "Public Drives," p. —). A very pleasant route in the summer season is by the Harlem boats from Fulton slip or Peck slip to Harlem Bridge; thence by small steamer to High Bridge. Fare to Harlem 10 cents; thence to the Bridge — cents. Harlem may also be reached by the Second, Third and Eighth avenue horse-cars. The sail up the Harlem River on the little steamer is a very charming one. The surrounding scenery is fine, and the Bridge is constantly in view. Arrived at the Bridge, good hotels and delightful walks and drives will be found. The Bridge is built of granite, and is 1,450 feet long, and rests upon semi-circular arches which are supported by fourteen piers of substantial masonry. Eight of these arches have a span of 80 feet and six of 50 feet. The height is 114 feet above the ordinary high-water line of the river. Between the parapets the water pipes, properly protected from frost, are laid, and over all is a magnificent promenade for pedestrians.

§ 3. The Old Receiving Reservoir in Central Park.

This reservoir is 1,826 feet long and 836 feet wide, and including its embankments, contains 35.05 acres, and its area at the top-water line, 31 acres, divided into two divisions; the northern divison is designed to contain 20 feet depth of water, and the southern 30 feet in depth. But they are not fully excavated in some parts, where rock occurs, it not being deemed sufficiently important to incur the expense of excavation in rock for the increased capacity that would be obtained. The reservoir has a capacity for 150,000,000 imperial gallons. The reservoir is formed with earth banks, the interior having regular puddled walls to render them impervious to water; the outside protected by a stone wall, laid upon a slope of one horizontal to three vertical, the face laid in cement mortar and the inside dry; the inside is protected by a dry slope wall, laid on the face of the embankment, which slopes $1\frac{1}{2}$ horizontal to one vertical. The embankments are raised four feet above the top of water line, and are 18 feet wide on the top, excepting the high banks on the southern division and the western bank of the northern division, which are 21 feet wide. The greater part of the embankments for the northern division are of moderate height; but a portion of the eastern and western banks of the southern division are 38 feet high above their base. Vaults or brick archways are constructed, in which iron pipes are laid, so arranged that the pipes from the northern division connect with those from the southern division, and thence pass off to the distributing reservoir, and to supply the adjacent districts.

The main vault is on the eastern side; it is 540feet long and is 16 feet span; that on the western side is 400 feet in length, and 8 feet span; designed for supplying at a future day the districts on the North river side above Forty-second street. The pipes are all provided with stop-cocks, and so arranged that they can receive the water from either division; except one pipe from each division, that leads to the distributing reservoir. It carries three lines of pipes to the distributing reservoir, and the arrangement allowing two pipes to be drawn from either division, so that in the event of emptying one of the divisions for repairs, the other would supply two pipes for the distributing reservoir, and all other pipes having a connection with each division would be in full supply, notwithstanding the suspension of one division. A pipe is put through the division bank, with a stop-cock, to allow the water or not, as may be desired, to pass from one division to the other.

The aqueduct intersects the reservoir at right angles with its westerly line, and 252 feet south of the northwesterly corner.

At this point a gate-chamber is constructed, with one set of gates to pass the water into the northern division and another set to pass it into a continued conduit of masonry constructed within the embankment of the reservoir to the angle of the southern division, where it enters by a brick sluice into this division.

This arrangement gives the power of directing the water into either division, or both, at the same time, as may be desired.

In the division bank, a waste weir is constructed to carry off the surplus water from either division, when it rises to the proper height.

§ 4. The New Receiving Reservoir in Central Park.

The new Reservoir is a vastly larger work than the old one, and was only completed in the autumn of 1861. The water was formally introduced April 19, 1862. It is north of the old Reservoir, and extends from 86th to 96th streets, and is of nearly the whole width of the park. The total area is 106 acres, and its capacity is one thousand millions of gallons.

§ 5. The Distributing Reservoir.

This reservoir is on the west side of Fifth avenue, extending from Fortieth to Forty-second streets. It is built in the Egyptian style of architecture with massive buttresses. Its form is square, and it measures 420 feet on each side. It has an area of four acres, and like the Receiving Reservoir, is separated into two divisions. It occupies the highest ground in the vicinity, and is higher than any other part of the city south of it. It has an average elevation of 45 feet above the neighboring streets, and a capacity to contain 20,000,000 imperial gallons. It is designed for 36 feet of water, and when full will stand 115 feet above mean tide. The walls rise four feet above the water line. Upon the top is a fine promenade, to which the visitor will find ready access, and from which he will obtain a fine view of the city and surrounding country.

[The Fifth avenue and Fulton Ferry line of omnibuses pass the Reservoir every few minutes.]

CHAPTER VII.

NOTABLE STREETS AND SIGHTS.

1. Broadway.—2. Wall Street.—3. Fifth Avenue.—4. The Bowery.—5. The Slums.

§ 1. Broadway.

[The visitor will receive material assistance in finding his way about the city, or recovering it when lost, by observing the corner street-lamps. Two of these lamps at the intersection of every two streets have the names of the streets conspicuously painted on them.]

Broadway, as everybody knows, is the principal street in the city. It runs the whole length of the island, and forms its backbone. From the Battery to Union Square, a distance of two miles and a half, for the most part of the day, its sidewalks and shop windows present a panorama which, for beauty, variety, and interest, is scarcely to be paralleled in the world. The throng of people on the walks, the rush of vehicles in the street, the bustle and noise which greet one's ears, are sufficient to make a nervous person wish himself a thousand miles away; and yet, without Broadway, New York would lose a large part of its attractions for the stranger. All the great retail shops seek Broadway, and many of the wholesale ones. Here are Stewart's, McCreery's, Lord & Taylor's, and Arnold & Constable's, among the dry goods trade; Ball, Black & Co., and Tiffany & Co. of the jewelers; Appleton's and Scribner's of the book-sellers, not to mention hundreds of others. Many of the leading hotels, too, are on Broadway; the Astor, St. Nicholas, Metropolitan, Grand Central, Fifth Avenue, the Hoffman, St. James, Coleman, Gilsey and Grand hotels, etc., etc. In the lower part, wholesale stores, banks and insurance offices predominate. Prominent among these, and worthy of notice, are the Park Bank, opposite St. Paul's church; the "Herald" office adjoining; the Equitable Life Insurance building, corner of Cedar st.; the N. Y. Life Insurance building, corner of Leonard st., and the new stores corner of Warren st, and those at the corner of Park Place. It was said by a shrewd

New York politician, years ago, that it required more talent to cross Broadway at Fulton street without getting one's neck broke than it did to get to be a member of Congress! But for the benefit of the nervous stranger we will advise him that he will now find, during the busy hours of the day, a policeman at that point, whose duty it is to see him safely across the street, and, however intricate the path may seem to be or desperate the undertaking, he will do it. At this point the visitor will find himself in front of *Saint Paul's church* (Episcopal), and grave-yard. In a niche over the portico is a small figure of Saint Paul, and below in the front is a rural monument to *Gen. Montgomery*, who fell at the storming of Quebec. On the Vesey st. side of the yard is a monument to *Dr. McNevin*, a distinguished Irish patriot of '98, for many years a practicing physician of the city; on the other side there is one to *Thomas Addis Emmett*, another Irish exile, and brother of the celebrated Robert Emmett. Between the Battery and Union Square there remain at present, but three churches, Trinity, St. Paul's and Grace. This last is a beautiful edifice and spire, near Tenth street, which may be seen for a long distance, up and down the street. Above Union Square, Broadway for a long distance, presents the same general features; elegant stores and immense stocks of the finest goods, invite the attention of all passers-by.

§ 2. Wall Street

Is scarcely a quarter of a mile in length, but it is the great money centre of the country, and its influence is potent in every quarter of the globe where mercantile transactions are known. Few strangers visit the city who have not some business to transact in Wall st., and those who have none, will do well to visit the street during the busy hours of the day, say from 12 M. to 3 P. M. One line of Broadway omnibuses passes through the street, and three other lines pass the head of the street at Trinity church every few minutes, rendering it easy of access from all parts of the city. Several of the public buildings elsewhere described, are in this street, but besides these, there are many other buildings, banks, insurance offices, banking offices, and stores in the street, or in its immediate vicinity, well worthy of notice. See, for instance, the new Seamen's Bank for Savings, corner Wall and Pearl; the Bank of New York, corner Wall and William; and the banking-house of Brown Brothers & Co., 59 Wall st. But what will attract the attention of the visitor more than anything else will be the rushing of men and boys in and out of offices and through the street; the haste with which everybody seems to be infected; the anxiety stamped on every one's face; the clicking of the telegraph in almost every office you pass; the knots of men on the street corners talking and gesticulating like mad, and the screaming bedlam of the Gold Exchange. If the visitor has not been accustomed to noise and bustle in other places, the hour he spends here will seem to be tripled, and he will soon wish himself out of it. It is, however, one of the city's most interesting features, and no stranger should go away without visiting it.

§ 3. Fifth Avenue.

Fifth Avenue is the "west end" of New York city. It begins at Washington Square, and ends at Harlem river, and is about midway between the North and East rivers. It is built up continuously between three and four miles, and on it reside many of the city's wealthiest families whose houses are far more elegant and costly than can be found in any other city in the country. Could the stranger obtain entrance into some of these dwellings, he would be astonished at the evidences of wealth and culture that would meet his eye. Probably the most expensive, and by far the most luxurious residence on the avenue, is that of Mr. A. T. Stewart, corner of Thirty-fourth st. It as far exceeds those of his neighbors, as his dry goods palace, corner of Broadway and Tenth st., does those of the other dry goods merchants. This house is said to have cost more than two millions of dollars. The visitor, if he is a careful observer, will note the changes in the style of building as he wends his way up the avenue.

Houses which were considered to be "just the thing" ten years ago, are out of date to-day. Observe the style of the houses about Fourteenth st., for instance; then at Twenty-fifth to Thirtieth streets, and again, those which are now being erected ten or twenty streets farther up. Between Fifty-fifth and Fifty-sixth streets, for example, a block of houses has just been built of Ohio stone—a material fast coming into use, and destined to supplant brownstone. These houses are finished with mansard roofs, and are vastly more attractive than the houses of ten years ago. The visitor will notice a new feature of the fashionable house of to-day, that the inside wood-work as well as the outside doors, are of mahogany. Another block that will attract attention is just finished, between Fifty-seventh and Fifty-eighth streets. These houses are of white marble, and when one is a little distance away, the effect has been so contrived that the block may very well be mistaken for a church. On that portion of the avenue which is on Central Park, fabulous prices have been obtained for building lots, the position being beyond all question the finest in the city. Some of the most fashionable churches are located on this avenue, and if the visitor should be in the city of a Sunday, he is recommended to take a walk on this popular promenade after the morning services are over, if he would see one of the city's most elegant and characteristic exhibitions. The churches most worthy of notice on the avenue are *St. Thomas's*, corner of Fifty-third street; the *Jewish Temple*, corner of Forty-third street; the *Roman Catholic Cathedral* (now building), between Fifty-first and Fifty-second streets, and *Dr. Chapin's Church*, corner of Forty-fifth st.

Several of the old and wealthy club houses are on this avenue, and on the corner of Fourteenth street is Delmonico's celebrated restaurant. We already begin to see houses converted into stores in the lower portion of the avenue and business driving residences further away.

A man need not be more than sixty years old to remember when the Battery was, to the fashionable world, what Fifth avenue and Fiftieth street are to-day. If this old fellow should live twenty-five years longer where shall he look to find the centre of fashion?

§ 4. The Bowery

Is by no means a fashionable promenade. Still it is worth one's while to see it, especially of an evening. It has always been a great thoroughfare, and remains so still. That portion of the city east of the Bowery is largely inhabited by Germans, and on the Bowery are a great number of the most extensive lager bier saloons in the city, a German theatre, concert saloons, etc., etc. Besides these, however, are a large number of retail shops, all of which are open and brilliantly lighted in the evening. The Bowery begins at Chatham Square, and extends to the Cooper Institute at the junction of Third and Fourth avenues. The Bowery Theatre is an object of interest, too. Scarcely any one would believe that this was once a fashionable theatre; that Malibran sang there; that Gilfert was the manager; that its boxes were thronged with the élite of New York, and the streets in that neighborhood with their carriages! But that was forty years ago! Some half a dozen theatres which have stood on this place have been burned. The present building has stood longer than any of its predecessors. Next door to the theatre is the attraction which will prove the strongest, probably, for the stranger. This is the Atlantic Garden, the greatest German lager-bier saloon of the city. If you have not been there, reader, go there some Saturday evening if you can, and you will get an idea of the way the Germans enjoy themselves, and you will see sights that will be new to you.

"St. Mark's Church in the Bouerie," as it is called, though not in the Bowery as we know it to-day, was so, when it was built, in 1799, when it must have been a long distance from the city. The old Stuyvesant mansion was then standing, and the "Bouerie Lane" and the old Boston Road were the nearest highways. It was in this mansion that Peter Stuyvesant spent the later years of his life. His remains were buried in a vault in St. Mark's Church. The church stands in what is now called Stuyvesant street near the Second ave.

§ 5. The Five Points.

This chapter would hardly be complete without some directions by which a stranger, who was so inclined, might be able to see the lowest depths of the city without running much risk of either life or limb. To any one who has plenty of nerve, who is not sensitive to offensive smells, and who wishes to see the foulest and most repulsive sights, we advise that he make up a party, and get his landlord or some friend to secure the services of a policeman for the night, who is accustomed to go on these expeditions. Before going out, empty your pockets of everything valuable, and take a bottle of smelling salts with you. Tell your policeman where you want to go and what you desire to see. If you have read Dickens's American Notes, you will have some idea of what is before you; if you have not, you will, probably, after you have been through, around and under the Five Points at night.

CHAPTER VIII.
PLACES OF AMUSEMENT.

1. Booth's Theatre—2. Grand Opera House—3. Academy of Music—4. Wallack's—5. Fifth Avenue Theatre—6. Fourteenth Street Theatre—7. Olympic—8. The Globe—9. Niblo's Garden—10. Wood's Museum—11. Bowery Theatre—12. Stadt Theatre—13. Union Square Theatre—14. Lent's Circus.

§ 1. **Booth's Theatre.**

(Cor. Sixth Avenue and Twenty-third Street).

This theatre is one of the architectural ornaments to the city; and, taken as a whole in all its appointments, it is the most elegant and the best contrived theatre in the whole country. Its two fronts are built of New Hampshire granite, and the edifice is in the Renaissance style of architecture. The front on Twenty-third street is 150 feet; on the avenue, 100; and the height is 95 feet. The stage is 75x55 feet. On the Twenty-third street front are three large doors which can be instantly opened in case of fire; affording ample facility for emptying the house of spectators in five minutes.

ACCESS.—The Sixth Avenue cars, and the Broadway and 23d street line of omnibuses pass the theatre every few minutes.

ADMISSION, $1.00; reserved seats, $1.50; family circle, 75c.

§ 2. **The Grand Opera House,**

(Cor. Eighth Avenue and Twenty-third Street).

This is an elegant and imposing edifice in the Italian style of architecture. Its two fronts are of white marble—that on the avenue is 115 feet in length; the one on Twenty-third street is 100 feet. The building seen from the street, however, is not the theatre; that is a separate building in the rear, to which the other supplies means of ingress and egress. The main entrance is on the avenue; it is spacious and leads by a grand stairway to an immense vestibule, from which smaller stairways lead directly into the theatre. The interior is very handsome, and is admirably arranged with capacity to seat a very large audience. The stage is unusually large, and is provided with all the appliances for the production of showy spectacles.

Access:—The Eighth Avenue cars, and the Broadway and 23d street line of omnibuses pass the door every few minutes.

Admission, $1.00; reserved seats, $1.50; family circle, 50c.

§ 3. **The Academy of Music,**

(Cor. Fourteenth Street and Irving Place).

This is the opera house proper of the city. It is a large and unpretending building, with a very elegant interior. It was intended for musical purposes, but for several years the Italian opera has not been a success, and it is now frequently used for public meetings, when a large place is wanted.

Access:—It is one block east of Fourth avenue, on which there is a line of horse cars and an omnibus line; and one block west of the Third avenue cars. A crosstown horse car line passes the door.

Admission varies with the attraction.

§ 4. **Wallack's Theatre,**

(Cor. Broadway and Thirteenth Street).

For any one who appreciates a theatrical performance, in which the subordinate characters are counted for any thing more than sticks, Wallack's is the theatre to go to. The stock company at the regular theatrical season numbers among its members some actors and actresses who would be "stars" at most of the other theatres. It is an exceedingly comfortable, capacious, and well-arranged theatre, and their plays are always admirably put upon the stage.

Access:—The Broadway and Fourth avenue, and the Broadway and 23d street lines of omnibuses pass the door; and the Fourth avenue and the University Place lines of cars pass within one block of the theatre.

Admission, 75c., stalls, $1.50, family circle, 50c.

7*

§ 5. **Fifth Avenue Theatre,**
(No. 4 West Twenty-fourth Street.)

This is a very pretty theatre, and, in the manner of putting its plays on the stage, more nearly resembles Wallack's than any other theatre in the city. It usually has a good stock company.

ACCESS:—The Broadway and University Place cars, the 42d street and Grand street ferry cars, and the Broadway and Fifth avenue omnibuses pass the corner.

ADMISSION, $1.00; reserved seats, $1.50; family circle, 50c.

§ 6. **The Fourteenth St. Theatre,**
(On Fourteenth Street, between Fifth and Sixth Avenues),

Was originally the French Theatre. The whirligig of time has brought several changes to this theatre, and it has so far been considered "unlucky." Mr. Charles Fechter has now leased it, and it is said will soon open it with a new company, among whom is Miss Leclerc.

ACCESS:—The Sixth avenue line of cars, and the Broadway and Fifth avenue line of omnibuses pass the corner of the streets near the theatre.

ADMISSION, $1.00; reserved seats, $1.50.

§ 7. **The Olympic,**
(Broadway, between Houston and Bleecker Streets—East Side).

This theatre used to be known as "Laura Keene's" but it has borne its present name for several years. Under its new management, it is celebrated for its burlesques—such as "Humpty Dumpty," etc.; G. L. Fox being the great attraction.

ACCESS:—Most of the Broadway omnibuses pass the door, and the Bleecker street line of cars passes the corner above.

ADMISSION, 75c., reserved seats, $1.00; family circle, 50c.

§ 8. **The Globe,**

(Broadway, between Fourth Street and Astor Place),

Is a small affair in a building which was, formerly, the Church of the Messiah, (Dr. Osgood's).

ACCESS:—All the Broadway stages pass the door.

ADMISSION 50c.; reserved seats, $1.00.

§ 8. **Niblo's Garden,**

(Broadway, bet. Prince and Houston Streets).

There are but few New-Yorkers, or very few strangers, who have ever visited New York, who have not, at some period of their lives, been to Niblo's Garden. For many years the Ravels were the great attraction, and were there frequently—and everybody went to see them—and more recently "The Black Crook" and such-like spectacles have drawn everybody and his wife. The theatre is centrally located, is near to the hotels, and easily accessible from all parts of the city and its suburbs.

ACCESS:—All the Broadway lines of omnibuses pass the door, and the Bleecker street cars will leave passengers at the corner of Prince and Crosby streets.

ADMISSION, $1.00; reserved seats, $1.50; family circle, 50c.

§ 10. **Wood's Museum,**

(Broadway and Thirtieth Streets).

This establishment inherits all there was left of Barnum's Museum, which is the name only. Its attractions are theatrical almost entirely. They present some of their showy spectacles very creditably, and it is well attended.

ACCESS:—The Broadway and University Place, and the 42d street and Grand street ferry lines pass the door.

ADMISSION 30c.; to different circles, different prices.

§ 11. **The Bowery Theatre,**
(In the Bowery [West Side], bet. Bayard and Canal Streets).

This is now the oldest theatre in the city. The first theatre built on this site nearly fifty years ago, was destroyed by fire, and a similar fate has happened to some half dozen of its successors. It is frequented by the commoner classes, and for them it is a favorite resort. It is one of the sights a stranger should see, who wants to see life in New York in all its phases.

ACCESS:—The Second avenue, the Third avenue, and the yellow Bleecker street lines of cars pass its doors.

ADMISSION, from 15c. to $1.00.

§ 12. **The Stadt Theatre** (German).
(In the Bowery [East Side], bet. Bayard and Canal Streets).

This is the German Theatre of the city. It is nearly opposite the Bowery Theatre. It has a respectable exterior, and a large and well adapted interior. There is generally a good company, and the place is largely frequented by Germans.

ACCESS:—The Second avenue, the Third avenue, and the yellow Bleecker street lines of cars pass the doors.

ADMISSION, from 10c. to $3.00.

§ 13. **Union Square Theatre,**
(Cor. Broadway and Fourteenth Street).

This is a new theatre just completed on the site of the Union Place Hotel. The position is an admirable one for a theatre; very central, and readily accessible by horse cars and omnibuses from any part of the city. The interior is said to be very elegant and commodious.

ACCESS:—The Broadway and Fourth avenue, and the Broadway and 23d st. lines of omnibuses pass the doors, and the Fourth ave., and 42d st. and Grand st. ferry lines of cars pass very near the doors.

ADMISSION, from 15c. to $1.50.

§ 14. Lent's Circus,

(Fourteenth Street, bet. Third and Fourth Avenues—South Side).

ACCESS:—Fourth and Third avenues, and the 42d st. and Grand st. ferry lines of cars.

ADMISSION, 50c. and $1.00.

§ 15. Minstrels.

Bryant's Minstrels, 23d street, between Sixth and Seventh avenues.

Newcomb & Arlington s, 28th Street Opera House, corner Broadway and 28th street.

San Francisco Minstrels, 585 Broadway, opposite Metropolitan Hotel.

Tony Pastor's, 201 Bowery.

Kelley & Leon's, 720 Broadway.

A general theatre-ticket office is at 114 Broadway, basement, kept by PULLMAN, where tickets or reserved seats may be obtained at theatre prices; which will be convenient for business men who have no time to run around.

CHAPTER IX.

DRIVES.

1. To Jerome Park—2. To Kingsbridge—3. To Fordham—4. To Greenwood Cemetery—5. To Coney Island—6. To Staten Island.

For the great majority of travelers it would be unnecessary to give the drives described in this chapter. Central Park will afford driving ground enough. But occasionally a stranger would like to take a longer drive and to see more of the surrounding country. For the benefit of such strangers, therefore we give here several routes which are the favorite drives of those who keep good teams, and are fond of long drives.

§ 1. To Jerome Park.

Assuming a convenient point of departure, say corner of Fourteenth street and Fifth avenue, you drive by way of the avenue to Central Park; there take the East side drive to Sixth avenue, to 125th street, to Harlem bridge; cross the bridge, turn to the right to the Southern Boulevard and on to Fordham and Jerome Park. 12 miles.

Return. By Central avenue and High Bridge street to High Bridge; then back to Central avenue to Macomb's Dam, and by the lane to Eighth avenue, to St. Nicholas avenue, to Seventh avenue and to Central Park, and by the West side drive to Fifth avenue and Fourteenth street.

§ 2. To Kingsbridge.

By same route as the first to and through the Park, then to St. Nicholas avenue, to West side Boulevard on through Manhattanville, Carmansville, Fort Washington to Spuyten Duyvil and to Kingsbridge. 12 miles.

Return. Cross Kingsbridge and on by Central avenue as per route 1.

§ 3. To Fordham.

To Central Park and through it as in route 1, to St. Nicholas avenue, to Sixth avenue, to 125th street and to Harlem Bridge. Cross the bridge and go on by the old Boston post road via Melrose, and Tremont to Fordham.

RETURN. By the same route.

§ 4. TO GREENWOOD CEMETERY.

[Tickets of admission can be obtained at the office of the Cemetery Company, 30 Broadway, free of charge.]

Cross the South Ferry to Brooklyn, up Atlantic avenue which is paved with wood to Fourth avenue which is macadamised, to 24th or 25th streets, then turn to the left and you will see the entrance gate. Several hours will be occupied with the drive inside the cemetery, if the stranger desires to see all the works of art and the fine scenery of the place.

RETURN. Pass out of the cemetery by the gate back to Fourth avenue to Fifteenth street to Ninth avenue to the gate. Enter Prospect Park, and through the Park out by the Flatbush avenue gate, down the avenue to Livingston street, through that street to Clinton street, to Jerolamen street to Henry street, to Fulton street to the ferry.

§ 5. TO CONEY ISLAND.

Cross the Fulton ferry and up Henry street to Jerolamen to Clinton to Schemerhorn or Livingston to Flatbush avenue to the main entrance of Prospect Park; through the Park by main drive, to new Boulevard, thence by the Coney Island Road to the Island.

RETURN. By way of way of Bath, Fort Hamilton and Shore road to Bay Ridge to Fourth avenue, to Atlantic avenue to the ferry.

§ 6. TO STATEN ISLAND.

The finest drives around the city perhaps, are on Staten Island. No where else is there such variety in the scenery, nowhere else are there more elegant and expensive residences. The following will be found a delightful drive, and the visitor who drives out there once will probably not need urging to go again:

Leave the city by the North Shore Ferry, at Pier 19

N. R., land at New Brighton, or at West N. Brighton; take Richmond terrace to Davis or Bard avenue, to Castleton avenue to Serpentine road: cross Richmond Road at Silver Lake, follow Serpentine Road to Ocean View; passing the residences of Geo. Law, W. B. Duncan, E. Cunard, Dutihl, Brown, Jacob Vanderbilt and Van Duzer to Clove Road, follow Clove Road to Vanderbilt avenue, to Clifton, to Vanderbilt Landing and then take the other ferry to the city, landing at Whitehall.

CHAPTER X.

THE PUBLIC MARKETS.

There is little to be seen at any of the markets of the city to interest the stranger. The two principal markets, Washington and Fulton, are a couple of tumble-down shanties, encumbered with every nuisance which it is possible to concentrate around a market. If, however, the visitor should be interested in farm produce, and would like to see such quantities of it as he probably never dreamed of, he is recommended to rise early some Saturday morning and go down to Washington market. Go all through both the regular and the outside markets; then go around the intersecting streets for half a mile each way and count, if he can, the farmers' wagons he will find there, loaded down with produce; then let him calculate the quantity, and imagine where there are people enough to eat it all. The city markets are located as follows:

1. *Washington Market*, where a vast deal more produce is sold than any where else in the city, is on North River, at the foot of Vesey and Fulton streets.

2. *Fulton Market*, is on East River at the foot of Fulton and Beekman streets.

3. *Catherine Market*, is on the East River at the foot of Catharine street.

4. *Centre Market*, is on the block bounded by Grand, Centre, Broome and Baxter streets.

5. *Essex Market*, is on Grand and Ludlow streets.

6. *Tompkins Market*, is on Third avenue, East side, extending from 6th to 7th street.

7. *Jefferson Market*, is at the junction of Sixth and Greenwich avenues.

8. *Clinton Market*, is on North River foot of Canal and Spring streets.

9. *Franklin Market*, is on East River at Old Slip.

10. *Union Market*, is at the junction of Second and Houston streets.

11. *Governeur Market*, is on East River, corner of Water and Governeur streets.

CHAPTER XI.

PUBLIC LIBRARIES.

1. The Astor Library—2. The Mercantile Library—3. N. Y. Society Library—4. Library of the N. Y. Historical Society—5. Cooper Institute Library—6. The Apprentices' Library—7. The Law Library—8. The City Library—9. The Mott Memorial Free Medical Library—10. The Medical Library—11. The Printers' Library—12. The Woman's Library—13. Library of the Young Men's Christian Association.

§ 1. THE ASTOR LIBRARY

Is located in Lafayette Place, on the east side, between Fourth street and Astor Place, and is very near to Broadway. The present library building is about 150 feet wide and 100 feet deep. Its architecture is of the Byzantine order, with brown stone trimmings, and a handsome entablature. The rooms occupied by the library are on the second floor; they are spacious and well-lighted, and are reached by means of a fine marble staircase. The library numbers at present about 150,000 volumes; and, among them, are some of the rarest books to be found anywhere. It is open to the public—free to every one to consult or read its books—from 9 A.M. to 5 P.M., daily.

§ 2. THE MERCANTILE LIBRARY

Is located on Astor Place, between Broadway and Fourth avenue, and is the largest circulating library in the country, and has the largest income. It has branch offices at 76 Cedar street, 1456 Third avenue, and at Yonkers, Norwalk, Stamford, Elizabeth, Paterson, and Jersey City. It has a very large reading-room—better supplied, probably, with magazines, reviews, and papers than any other; the number at present being 452.

Strangers are allowed to consult books of reference in the alcoves of the library hall; and, if they should be introduced by a member, they will receive a card entitling them to the privileges of the reading-room for one month. It is open from 9 A.M. to 10 P.M.

§ 3. The Society Library

Is located at 67 University Place, east side, between 12th and 13th streets. It is, perhaps, the oldest public library in the United States. It was incorporated in the year 1700 under the name of "The Public Library of New York." In 1754, its corporate name was changed to "The New York Society Library." The building which belongs to the Society is about 50 feet front, very plain and unpretentious, but being designed for the library, is well adapted to its purpose. The number of volumes in this library is about 45,000. Some of them are very rare. The library is open week-days, from 8 A.M. till sunset, and the reading-rooms until 10 P.M. Twenty-five dollars is the fee for membership, and six dollars per annum, the dues.

Access:—The Broadway and University Place cars, and the Fulton ferry line of stages pass the library every few minutes.

§ 4. Library of the N. Y. Historical Society

Is located on Second avenue, corner of 11th street. This Society is in the possession of a large collection of rare books and manuscripts, pamphlets, maps, charts, and files of newspapers which, for historical purposes, are invaluable. Its rooms are open daily, and strangers are admitted on the introduction of a member.

§. 5 The Cooper Institute Library.

This, like the Astor Library, is a library of reference; books cannot be taken out, but both library and reading rooms are free to the public. The number of volumes in the library is limited, but additions are making to it all the time. The books are generally of a scientific character, and the reading-room is well supplied with magazines and newspapers. Open from 9 A.M. to 9 P.M.

§ 6. The Apprentices' Library.

This library is located at 472 Broadway, and numbers about 50,000 volumes—free to all apprentices whether male or female, who can bring a certificate of good character from parents, guardian, or employer. The library was founded by the "Society of Mechanics and Tradesmen."

§ 7. THE LAW LIBRARY.

This library is located at No. 41 Chambers street, and is open only to members.

§ 8. THE CITY LIBRARY

Is a very small collection of books kept at Room No. 12, City Hall. Open to the public, daily, from 10 A.M. to 4 P. M.

§ 9. THE MOTT MEMORIAL FREE MEDICAL LIBRARY

Is located at No. 64 Madison avenue and is intended mainly for the benefit of medical students. It has some 2,500 volumes on its shelves, and is open from 9 A.M. to 9 P.M.

§ 10. THE MEDICAL LIBRARY AND JOURNAL ASSOCIATION.

Is also at No 64 Madison avenue. The library numbers about 3000 volumes, chiefly medical—and they have a reading-room well supplied with the medical journals of this country and Europe. For members only. Open from 9 A.M. to 9 P.M.

§ 11. THE PRINTERS' LIBRARY.

The Printers' Society hold their meetings at No. 3 Chambers street, where they have collected a small library of miscellaneous books and books relating to the art of printing, which are free to the craft whether members of the Society or not. It is open only on Saturday afternoons.

§ 12. WOMAN'S LIBRARY

Is a young institution at No. 38 Bleecker street, especially intended to benefit women. It is open daily from 9 A.M. to 4 P.M.

§ 13. Library of the Y. M. C. Association.

Is the new building of the Association, corner Fourth and E. 24th street. The reading-rooms are very well supplied with papers and magazines, and with every other convenience necessary to render them attractive, especially to young men.

CHAPER XII.

PRINCIPAL CHURCHES IN THE CITY.

[STRANGERS who are in the city over Sunday will miss the Broadway omnibuses and the facility they afford for getting around the city. The street cars, however, run on Sundays, and by looking over the routes, the stranger will readily discover whether either of them will carry him to the particular church to which he desires to go. If for instance, the visitor wishes to go to Brooklyn to hear Mr. Beecher, by looking at the horse-car routes, p. 15, he will find that the Bleecker street cars run to Fulton Ferry; the Belt Line cars pass the ferry; the Second avenue line cars stop one block above the ferry. By the other lines one can come to the Park or Astor House; thence to the ferry via Fulton street is not a long walk. Cross the ferry, up Fulton street to Hicks, which is but a short distance, turn to the right, at the fourth street turn to the left, and you will find the church. An equally safe direction would be to follow the crowd from the ferry.

Services at Mr. Beecher's are held in the morning and evening at the usual hours.]

§ 1. Protestant Episcopal.

Trinity, Broadway, corner Rector, and opposite to Wall street.
St. Paul's, Broadway corner Fulton street.
St. John's, Varick street opposite H. R. R. Depot.
Grace, No. 800 Broadway.

St. George's, Rutherford Place, corner Sixteenth.
St. Bartholomew, Lafayette Place, cor. Gt. Jones st.
St. Thomas's, Fifth avenue corner 53d.
Trinity Chapel, No. 15 W. 25th.
St. Alban's, 47th street near Lexington avenue.
Transfiguration, East 29th street near Fifth avenue.
St. Mark's, Stuyvesant street, near Second avenue.
Du St. Esprit, (French) No. 30 West 22d.
Ascension, Fifth avenue corner W. 10th.

§ 2. Presbyterian.

Brick Church, corner Fifth avenue and W. 37th street.
Fifth avenue, corner E. 19th street.
First, corner Fifth avenue and W. 11th street.
Fourth avenue, No. 288 Fourth avenue.
Madison Square, Madison avenue, cor. E. 24th street.
Scotch, No. 53 W. 14th street.
Thirteenth street, No. 145 W. 13th street.
University Place, corner E. 10th street.
West. No. 31 W. 42d street.
French Evangelical, 9 University Place.
German, No. 290 Madison street.

§ 3. Baptist.

Amity street, W. 54th street near Eighth avenue.
Fifth avenue, No. 6 W. 46th street.
First, Park avenue, corner E. 39th street.
Madison avenue, corner E. 31st street.
Sixteenth street, No. 257 W. 16th street.
Stanton street, No. 36 Stanton street.
Tabernacle, No. 166 Second avenue.
Antioch, No. 278 Bleecker.
First German, E. 14th street near First avenue.

§ 4. Congregational.

Tabernacle, corner Sixth avenue and 34th street.
New England, Madison avenue corner E. 47th street.
Church of the Pilgrims, No. 365 W. 48th street.

§ 5. Friends' Meetings.

East Fifteenth, corner Rutherford Place.
Twentieth street, E. 20th street near Third avenue.
Twenty-seventh street, 43 W. 27th street.

§ 6. Jewish Synagogues.

The Temple, corner Fifth avenue and 43d street.
Shaari Tephila, No. 127 W. 44th street.
Shearith Israel, W. 19th street near Fifth avenue.
Bnai Jeshurum, No. 145 W. 34th street.
Shaari Zedeck, No. 38 Henry street.

§ 7. Methodist Episcopal.

Allen street, No. 126 Allen street.
Central, No. 58 Seventh avenue.
Washington Square, No. 137 W. 4th street.
Trinity, No. 248 W. 34th street.
Seventh street, No. 24 Seventh street, near Third ave.
St. Paul's, Fourth avenue corner E. 22d street.
Rose Hill, No. 221 E. 27th street.
Eighteenth street, No. 307 W. 18th street.
John street, No. 44 John between Nassau and William streets.
German, No. 252 Second street.

§ 8. Reformed Dutch.

North Dutch, William street corner of Fulton.
[This is the church in which the celebrated Fulton street week-day prayer meetings originated, and next door to the church, No. 103 Fulton street, they are still held every week day at 12 o'clock.]
Access. The Fifth avenue stages and the Bleecker st. cars pass the door. It is very near also to Broadway.
Lafayette Place, corner E. 4th street.
Fifth avenue, corner W. 29th street.
St. Paul's, W. 40th near Sixth avenue.
Washington Square, corner Washington Place.
South, Fifth avenue corner W. 21st street.

§ 9. Lutheran.

Holy Trinity, No. 47 W. 21st street.
St. James, No. 216 E. 15th street.
St. Luke's, No. 318 W. 43d street.
St. Matthew's, No. 354 Broome street.
St. Peter's, No. 45 E. 50th street.

§ 10. Roman Catholic.

St. Peter's, corner Barclay and Church streets.
St. Patrick's (cathedral) corner Mott and Prince.
St. Stephen's, No. 149 E. 28th street.
Holy Cross, 335 W. 42d street.
St. Ann's, No. 112 E. 12th street.
St. Francis Xavier, No. 36 W. 16th street.
St. Mary's, No. 438 Grand street.
St. Vincent de Paul, No. 127 W. 23d street.
St. Joseph's, Sixth avenue cor. Washington place.

§ 10. Unitarian.

All Souls', Tenth avenue corner 20th street.
Messiah, corner Park avenue and E. 34th street.

§ 11. Universalist.

Fourth, (Dr. Chapin's), corner Fifth av. and 43d st.
Third, Bleecker corner Downing.
Our Saviour, No. 65 W. 35th street.

§ 12. Reformed Presbyterian.

First, No. 123 W. 12th street.
Second, No. 167 W. 11th street.
Third, No. 238 W. 23d street.

CHAPTER XIII.
PUBLIC INSTITUTIONS.

The traveler who comes to the city by way of the East River will not fail to notice the elegant and extensive public buildings on Ward's, Randall's, and Blackwell's Islands, opposite the upper end of the island. These are all city institutions, such as Alms-houses, Hospitals, Nurseries, Penitentiary, Idiot asylum, Insane asylum, Inebriate asylum, Prisons, &c., &c.

They are all under the direction of the *Department of Charities and Correction*. Office, N. W. corner of Third avenue and 11th street.

Any stranger who may wish to visit either or all of these institutions, must call at the office of the Department, where he may obtain a pass, and learn on what day, and how, he can reach the particular institution.

CHAPTER XIV.

PICTURE GALLERIES AND ARTISTS' STUDIOS.

The National Academy of Design, corner of Fourth avenue and 23d street, holds the principal exhibition of pictures in the city. The Spring Exhibition opens usually in April and closes about July 4th. The Fall Exhibition opens in November, and there is sometimes an intermediate one in the summer. Admission, 25 cents. Season tickets, $1. Catalogues, 25 cents. The academy has schools for drawing from the antique and from the living model.

Goupil's—Knoelder's, corner Fifth avenue and 22d street. This establishment imports largely of pictures and engravings, and always has a large number of pictures by native and foreign artists for sale. A portion of their establishment is devoted to the exhibition of their best paintings, which is open at all times to the public, free.

Schaus's, 749 Broadway, opposite to Astor Place, is a establishment similar to Goupil's. There is always something there worth going to see.

Snedicor's, 768 Broadway, is another place where there are usually some good pictures.

At the rooms of *N. Y., Historical Society*, (Second avenue corner of 11th street,) there is a collection of pictures of considerable value; together with what is left of the celebrated collection of Egyptian curiosities made by Mr. Abbott. The stranger must obtain a card of admission from a member in order to see them.

THE ARTISTS' STUDIOS.

The studios of the principal artists of the city, are open to visitors generally during the Autumn and Winter months, on *Saturday afternoons*. We give herewith the location of the buildings where many of the studios will be found.

West Tenth street, between Fifth and Sixth avenues.

N. Y. University Building on Washington Square.
Somerville Building, cor. Fifth avenue and 14th st.
No. 212 Fifth avenue.
Broadway, corner of 30th street.
Corner of Broadway and 37th street.
Corner of Fourth avenue and 24th street.
N. Y. Y. M. C. A. building, Fourth av. and 23d st.
Dodworth's Building, 806 Broadway, and at 786 Broadway.

CHAPTER XV.

PRINCIPAL CHARITABLE INSTITUTIONS.

1. Institution for the Deaf and Dumb.—2. The Blind Asylum.—3. Bloomingdale Asylum for the Insane.—4. The Leake & Watts Orphan House.—5. N. Y. Orphan Asylum.—6. N. Y. Juvenile Asylum.—7. The Sailors' Snug Harbor.—8. Five Points House of Industry.

§ 1. INSTITUTION FOR THE DEAF AND DUMB.

This institution is located on the southern slope of Washington Heights, just above Carmansville. The buildings are spacious and so situated as to command a splendid view of the surrounding country. The grounds comprise some forty acres. Pupils of both sexes are received. Yearly expenses, $150.

ACCESS.—By Hudson River railroad to Carmansville depot.

§ 2. N. Y. INSTITUTION FOR THE BLIND.

This institution is located on the block bounded by Eighth and Ninth avenues and 33d and 34th streets.

Visitors are received on Tuesdays.

ACCESS.—By Eighth or Ninth avenue cars.

§ 3. BLOOMINGDALE ASYLUM FOR THE INSANE.

This institution is located between 115th and 120th streets, just below Manhattanville. The buildings are extensive and the grounds—about forty acres—are laid out with taste, and abound in shrubbery and flowers.

ACCESS.—By Eighth avenue horse-cars, or by Hudson River Railroad to Manhattanville.

§ 4. The Leake & Watts Orphan House.

Was founded in 1827 by a legacy of Mr. J. G. Leake. It is located on the block bounded by Ninth and Tenth avenues and 111th and 112th streets. The income of the institution is able to support two or three hundred orphans. Access.—By Eighth avenue cars.

§ 5. N. Y. Orphan Asylum

Is on the Bloomingdale Road, between 73d and 74th streets. Its grounds extend to the river and comprise about fifteen acres. It is supported by private bequests.

Visitors are received on week days.

Access.—By Eighth avenue cars.

§ 6. N. Y. Juvenile Asylum

Is located on 176th street, near Tenth avenue. This is one of the most useful institutions in the city. It is beautifully situated, enjoying a commanding view of the river and the surrounding country. A house of reception connected with this institution is at 61 W. 13th street.

Access.—By Hudson River Railroad to Fort Washington station.

§ 7. The Sailors' Snug Harbor.

Office 156 Broadway. The institution is at New Brighton, Staten Island. It has several fine buildings well located, with extensive grounds, roaming over which will always be seen a large number of "old salts."

Access.—The North Shore Staten Island Ferry, from Pier No. 19, N. R., to second landing.

§ 8. Five Points House of Industry.

As its name would intimate to any one who knows anything about New York, is located in the immediate vicinity of the most filthy and degraded neighborhood in the city. The building is at 155, 157 and 159 Worth street. The amount of good this institution has done in feeding the hungry and clothing the naked is incalcuaable. The house is well worth visiting, and is open during the day at all hours, to strangers.

Access.—It is a short distance distance east of Broadway, on Worth street. The Fourth avenue cars pass Worth street at Centre.

CHAPTER XVI.

COLLEGES—LITERARY AND MEDICAL.

1. Columbia College.—2. N. Y. University.—3. College of the City of New York.—4. N .Y. College of Physicians and Surgeons.—5. University Medical College.—6. Bellevue Medical College.—7. N. Y. Medical College and Hospital for Women.—8. The Homœpathic Medical College.—9. Eclectic Medical College.

COLUMBIA COLLEGE is now located on Fourth avenue and E. 49th street. It was for many years in Park Place. It was originally chartered by the British Government, under the title of "King's College;" the charter bearing date 1754. In 1784 its name was changed to Columbia College. Alexander Hamilton, John Randolph of Roanoke, De Witt Clinton, and many others of the leading men of this country have been among its graduates. In 1857 the College was removed to its present site. The Columbia College Law School is at 37 Lafayette Place.

N. Y. UNIVERSITY, on the east side of Washington Square, between Washington and Waverley Places, was founded in 1831. It has a Department of Law and one of Medicine. The present edifice is an elegant white marble building, which was completed in 1836. Besides accommodating the classes, it has a large and very fine chapel, which is generally used as a church on Sundays, and it also affords studios for a number of artists.

COLLEGE OF THE CITY OF NEW YORK.—This institution, formerly the Free Academy, is located on Lexington avenue and 23d street. It is intended only for the graduates of the public schools, and was established in 1847.

MEDICAL COLLEGES.

NEW YORK COLLEGE OF PHYSICIANS AND SURGEONS, is on Fourth avenue, corner E. 23d street, and is the oldest Medical College in the city. It has a good library and physiological museum, and among its graduates will be found the names of some of the most distinguished physicians in the country.

UNIVERSITY MEDICAL COLLEGE, is connected with the N. Y. University, but is located at the Bellevue Hospital, at the foot of E. 26th street. It ranks among the highest medical schools, and graduates a large class every year.

BELLEVUE HOSPITAL MEDICAL COLLEGE, is also at the foot of E. 26th street.

THE NEW YORK MEDICAL COLLEGE AND HOSPITAL FOR WOMEN, is located at 187 Second avenue, and graduates a class of female physicians every year.

THE HOMŒPATHIC MEDICAL COLLEGE is at 151 E. 20th street, and the ECLECTIC MEDICAL COLLEGE at 223 E. 26th street.

CHAPTER XVII.

PRINCIPAL CEMETERIES IN AND AROUND THE CITY.

1. Greenwood Cemetery.—2. Cypress Hills Cemetery.—3. Cemetery of the Evergreens.—4. Trinity Cemetery.—5. The Marble Cemetery in Second street.—6. Calvary Cemetery.

§ 1. GREENWOOD CEMETERY.

This cemetery was incorporated in 1838. It is the most extensive and most beautiful burying-ground in the country. Its area is 413 acres. Length of drives is 17 miles; of foot-paths, 76 miles. It is located in South Brooklyn, about three miles from Fulton ferry, and two and a half from South ferry. The grounds are undulating, and at some points offer some of the finest views of the harbor, the ocean, islands and other surrounding scenery, which are to be had anywhere about; and this cemetery furnishes one of the finest drives around the city.

ACCESS.—By horse-cars from Fulton, Wall street, or South ferries.

§ 2. CYPRESS HILLS CEMETERY

Is located on that elevated ridge of land on the north side of the Brooklyn and Jamaica turnpike, usually known as "the back-bone of Long Island." Its distance from the Williamsburgh ferries is about five miles, and from the Brooklyn ferries about six miles. No location in the vicinity of New York embraces a greater variety of landscape, or more splendid and picturesque views. The carriage roads laid out and projected have an extent of over fifty miles. Its area is between three and four hundred acres.

Access.—By horse-cars from Brooklyn or Williamsburg to East New York, where omnibuses will be found to take visitors to the ground. Visitors going in their own conveyances are recommended to cross by the Williamsburg ferries, there inquire the best road to the *Williamsburg and Cypress Hills Macadamized road* which runs from Williamsburg to the New Western entrance, passing by the great Reservoir of the Brooklyn water-works.

§ 3. Cemetery of the Evergreens

Is on the Bushwick road, about three miles east of Brooklyn. The grounds possess many natural advantages for the purpose for which they are used, and the cemetery is one of the largest around the city.

Access.—By horse-cars from Williamsburg or Brooklyn to East New York.

§ 4. Trinity Cemetery

Is on the upper end of the Island, extending from 153d to 155th streets; its western boundary being the Hudson River Railroad. The grounds are beautifully situated and have been laid out with great taste. The remains of Audubon, the naturalist, repose in this cemetery.

Access.—By Hudson River Railroad to Carmansville station.

§ 5. Marble Cemetery in Second Street.

Almost the last remaining burial-place within the city proper, is the Marble Cemetry in Second street, between First and Second avenues, north side. It is a pretty little spot laid out and ornamented with good taste, and in its vaults repose the remains of many whose names have been honored in the city.

ACCESS.—The Broadway and Jesey City ferry omnibuses pass it; and the Second avenue cars pass the corner next to it.

§ 6. CALVARY CEMETERY.

THIS is the principal Cemetery consecrated to the Roman Catholics. It lies between East Brooklyn and Newtown, is prettily situated and tastefully laid out.

ACCESS.—By horse cars from South Seventh st. ferry.

CHAPTER XVIII.

DEPARTURE OF COASTWISE AND RIVER STEAMERS & THEIR RATES OF FARE.

FOR NEW ORLEANS.

The Merchants' Steamship Line.—Every Saturday at 3 P. M., from Pier 12. N. R.. office, No. 40 Broadway. Cabin Passage, $50; Steerage, $25.

The Cromwell Line.—Every Saturday from Pier 9, N. R., office 86 West street. Cabin Passage, $50; Steerage, $25.

Southern Line.—Every other Saturday from Pier 21, E. R., office 153 Maiden Lane. Cabin passage, $50; Steerage, $25.

FOR GALVESTON.

The Texas Line.—Weekly from Pier 20, E. R., office 153 Maiden Lane. Cabin passage, $65; Steerage, $35.

FOR KEY WEST.

The Texas Line.—The steamers for Galveston touch at Key West. Cabin passage, $40; Steerage, $25.

FOR SAVANNAH.

Atlantic Coast Mail Steamship Line.—Thursdays from

Pier 36, N. R., office corner Reade and West streets. Cabin passage, $20; Deck, $10.

Black Star Independent Line.—Saturdays from Pier 13 N. R., office 93 West street. Cabin passage, $20; Deck, $10.

Empire Line.—Saturdays at 3 P. M., from Pier 8, N. R., office No. 5 Bowling Green. Cabin passage, $20; Steerage, $10.

Murray's Line.—Thursdays at 3 P. M., from Pier 16, E. R., office No. 62 South street. Cabin passage, $20; Deck, $10.

FOR CHARLESTON.

New York and Charleston Steamship Company.—Tuesdays, Thursday and Saturdays at 3 P. M., from Pier 5, N. R., office corner West and Warren streets. Cabin passage, $20; Deck, $12.

FOR NORFOLK AND RICHMOND.

Old Dominion Steamship Company.—Tuesdays, Thursdays and Saturdays from Pier 37, N. R., office 187 Greenwich street. Passage to Norfolk $10, to Richmond $12, including meals and room.

FOR BOSTON.

Fall River and Newport Line.—Daily from foot of Chambers street, ticket office on the dock. Fare $5; meals and state-room extra.

Stonington Line.—On week days at 5 P. M., from Pier 33, N. R. Fare $5; meals and state-room extra.

Norwich and Worcester Line.—On week days at 5 P. M., from Pier 40, N. R. Fare $5; meals and state-room extra.

[Late in the Autumn the Boston boats change their hour of departure from 5 P. M. to 4 P. M.]

FOR PROVIDENCE.

Neptune Line of Steamers.—On week days at 5 P. M., from Pier 27, N. R. Fare to Providence, $3; meals and state-room extra.

FOR HARTFORD.

New York and Hartford Steamboat Line.—Week days at 4 P. M., from Peck Slip, E. R. Fare $1.50; meals and state-room extra.

FOR NEW HAVEN.

New York and New Haven Steamboat Line.—At 3:15 P. M., and at 11 P. M., on week days from Peck Slip, E. R. Fare, $1.25; meals and state-room extra.

FOR ALBANY.

Day Boats.—Daniel Drew and Chauncey Vibbard, at 8:45 A. M., from Pier 39, N. R. Fare, $2.00; meals extra.

Peoples' Line, Evening Boats.—St. John and Drew at 6 P.M., from Pier 41, N.R. Fare, $2.00; meals and state-room extra.

The Mary Powell.—For Rondout and intermediate landings at 3:50 P. M., from Pier 39, N. R.

CHAPTER XIX.

PRINCIPAL RAILROAD STATIONS AND HOW TO FIND THEM.

1. The N. Y. and New Haven, N. Y. and Harlem, and the Hudson River Railroads have the New Depot in common at 42d street and Fourth avenue.*

Access.—The Fourth avenue cars, and the Broadway and Fourth avenue omnibuses.

2. The Morris and Essex, the Delaware and Lackawana, and the Bloomfield and Montclair Railroad Depots are at Hoboken.

Access.—Ferry-boats from foot of Barclay and Christopher streets.

---

* Owing to some blundering on the part of the engineers in building the road connecting the Hudson River Railroad with the Harlem, the trains on the former road will not be able to come to the new depot at present. New York, Oct. 2.

3. The Erie R. R., the Northern New Jersey, and the Hackensack R. R. Depots are at Long Dock, Pavonia, Jersey City.

ACCESS.—Ferries from foot of Chambers street and foot of 23d street.

4. The New Jersey R. R. Depot is at Jersey City.

ACCESS.—Ferries from foot of Cortlandt street and Desbrosses street.

5. The New Jersey Central R. R. is at Communipaw.

ACCESS.—By ferry from foot of Liberty steet.

6. South Side, Long Island R. R. Depot is at Williamsburg.

ACCESS.—By ferries from foot of Roosevelt and Grand streets.

7. Long Island R. R. Depot is at Long Island City.

ACCESS.—By ferry from James slip and from 34th st.

CHAPTER XX.

THE SUBURBS.

§ 1. BROOKLYN.

BROOKLYN, the city of churches, the third city in point of population, the principal suburb of New York, contains more than 400,000 inhabitants; and Brooklyn people believe, that ere many decades elapse, their city will be more populous than New York. The following table shows its growth:

Years.	Population.	Years.	Population.
1802	86	1840	36,233
1814	3,805	1845	59,574
1816	4,492	1850	96,838
1820	7,475	1855	205,250
1825	10,795	1860	266,714
1830	15,295	1865	296,112
1835	24,310	1870	406,097

as every one knows, probably, Brooklyn is a city of

dwelling-houses, occupied by people who do business in the city of New York. It is more readily accessible to the lower portion of the city than the upper part of the Island is, and house-rent is cheaper. It counts among its attractions a large number of churches, with some few very distinguished clergymen, and a larger number of very sensational ones. It has a very fine opera house, several theatres, and is just completing an art-building which, for architectural beauty, will compare favorably with any building in the country. Prospect Park, about two-thirds the size of Central Park, has a location which commands far more extensive and picturesque views than are to be had at the latter Park; and Washington Park, the late Fort Greene, is a beautiful little breathing place. Greenwood cemetery, elsewhere described, is one of Brooklyn's chief attractions. Its Mercantile Library on Montague street, and the Long Island Historical Library, corner of Court and Jerolamen streets are thriving institutions, have a large number of members and readers, and offer all the attractions common to first-class libraries. Another of Brooklyn's attractions is

THE NAVY YARD.

This is a place of interest to many travelers, and the Brooklyn yard is one of the best appointed in the country. It is located on Wallabout bay, about a mile from Fulton ferry. Cars from this ferry pass the Yard, which is open to visitors daily from 10 A. M. to 3:30 P. M. On Tuesdays and Fridays visitors may be admitted on board the Receiving Ship.

Brooklyn now embraces what used to be known as Williamsburg. Travelers approaching New York by any of the principal lines will find that the Baggage Expressmen will take their baggage to any part of Brooklyn, and by reference to p. 10 they will learn the rates.

ACCESS.—Passengers arriving or departing by steamboat will find the Belt Railroad convenient. From the Forty-second street Depot, the Fourth avenue omnibus line ruus to South Ferry; the Madison avenue line to Wall street ferry; the Fifth avenue line to Fulton ferry.

STATEN ISLAND

Is, at its nearest point, about five miles south of the city. It is about fifteen miles long, from two to six wide, and is divided into several townships. The surface is undulating and from some parts the views to be obtained are magnificent. There are a large number of elegant residences on the island and several villages. Like all the suburbs of the city, the population is rapidly increasing.

ACCESS.—By ferries. The *North Shore ferry* from Pier No. 19, N. R., goes to New Brighton, West New Brighton, Port Richmond, and Elm Park. The other ferry is from foot of Whitehall street, and goes to the East Side, to Quarantine Landing, to Stapleton, and Vanderbilt's Landing, and connects with the Staten Island Railroad.

JERSEY CITY.

Jersey City is an important suburb of New York. It is the throroughfare by railroad to the South and West and is connected with New York by several ferries. The population in 1870, was 84,546, made up, like Brooklyn of New Yorkers almost exclusively. Within a few years the increase in population on the Jersey side by emigration from New York has been enormous. Villages on the line of the different railroads have sprung up like mushrooms, in a night.

HOBOKEN

Which a few years ago was merely a little hamlet, and was frequented only as romantic place for a Sunday afternoon walk, has fallen into line with all the other suburbs of New York, and has sprung into the proportions of a city. Two important railways have their depots here, and the Hamburgh and Bremen lines of steamers sail from her docks. Population in 1870, 20.297.

GOVERNOR'S ISLAND

Is a military station of some importance, and may be reached by ferry from foot of Whitehall street every hour from 8 A. M. to 6 P. M. Fare 15 cents. The last boat leaves the Island after evening parade.

CHAPTER XXI.

FOREIGN TRAVEL.

1. List of Foreign Consuls.—2. Steamers to foreign ports; their days of sailing, etc.

§ 1. PASSPORTS.

[Are issued by the Department of State free of expense, on application properly made. The applicant must, however, make his application in regular form, and it must be sworn to before a notary public. Notaries public are supplied with these forms and will fill them up and obtain passports for a fee of *two dollars*. If the applicant should not be known to the Notary, he must find some one to identify him. If he procures his own blank, and fills it properly, he can save something, but he must swear to it before a Notary, who is entitled therefor, to a fee of *twenty-five cents*.]

The traveler intending to go out of the country should provide himself with a passport from the State Department, which he can obtain without charge. Although he may never have occasion to show it, it might happen from contingencies which cannot be foreseen, to be indispensable. He should then procure from well known and responsible bankers, letters of credit on their correspondents at the principal city to which he may be going. It is convenient also to provide a small supply of pocket money in the coin of the country to which he may be going. Take as little baggage as possible; the great mistake Americans who go abroad make, is to take too much baggage.

In order to aid the traveler who is going abroad, we give a list of Foreign Consuls residing in the city and their places of business, and a list of steamers to foreign ports; their days of sailing; the piers from which they sail; the offices for securing passage; and the rates of fare.

§ 2. List of Foreign Consuls in New York City.

Argentine Republic—E. F. Davidson, 128 Pearl.
Austria—C. Boleslawski, 33 Broad.
Baden—L. Schmidt, 68 Broadway.
Bavaria—George H. Siemon, 85 Nassau.
Belgium—Chare's H. Mali, 45 Worth.
Bolivia—J. M. Munoz 63 Pine.
Brazil—Louis H. F. D'Aguiar, 13 Broadway.
Chile—Stephen Rogers, 249 W. 42d.
Colombia—Juan de Dios Restrepo, 25 William.
Costa Rica—A. C. Garcia, 19 Broad.
Denmark—C. T. Christensen, 112 Front, Henry Braem, V. C.
Dominica—D. A. De Lima, 23 William.
Ecuador—Nicholas R. Ansado, 7 Broadway.
France—Bellaigue de Bughas, acting ; George Kobb, V. C., 4 Bowing Green.
Great Britain—E. M. Archibald ; Pierrepont Edwards, V. C., 17 Broadway.
Greece—D. N. Botassi, 47 Exchange pl.
Guatemala—B. Blanco, 13 S. William.
Haiti—C. A. Vanbokkelen, 29 Front.
Hawaiian Islands—S. U. F. Odell, 24 Beaver.
Hesse—Darmstadt—F. W. Kentgen, 58 Beaver.
Honduras—E. G. Squier, Res. Min. 189 E. 39th.
Italy—Ferdinando de Luca; A. P. Bajnotti. V. C., 7 Broadway.
Liberia—H. M. Schieffelin, 42 Bible h.
Mexico (Republic)—Juan Navarro, 52 Exchange pl.
Monaco—H. Rouhaud, 2 Bowling gr.
Netherlands—R. C. Burlage ; J. E. Zimmerman, V. C., 45 Exchange pl.
Nicaragua—
North German Union—Johannes Roesing ; W. Zach, V. C., 117 B'way
Norway—C. Bors, 18 Exchange pl.
Paraguay—R. Mullowney, 91 Wall.
Peru—J. C. Tracy, 26½ Broadway.
Portugal—Antonio M. da Cunha Pereira de Sotto Maior; L. E. Amsinck. V. C., 148 Pearl.
Russia—R. Ostensacken, 52 Exchange pl.; R. Schultz, V. C., 25 Old sl
Salvador—Jose Jerman Ribon, 63 Pine.
Spain—Hipolito de Uriarte; F. Granados, V. C., 29 Broadway.
Sweden—C. Bors, 18 Exchange pl.
Switzerland—Louis P. Luze.
Turkey—C. Oscanyan, 66 Broadway.
Uruguay—Edwin C. B. Garsia, 19 Broad.
Venezuela—T. Hernandez, 121 Front.
Wurtemberg—Leopold von Bierwirth, 69 Pine.

§ 3. Foreign Steamers—Their Sailing Days ; from what Piers ; Business Offices ; Rates of Passage.

FOR LIVERPOOL.

CUNARD LINE.—Every Wednesday for steamers not carrying steerage passengers, from Jersey City, office No, 4 Bowling Green. Fare by the Scotia and the Russia, $130 gold, 1st cabin; $80 gold, 2d cabin. For the other Wednesday steamers, $100 gold, 1st cabin; $80 gold, 2d cabin. Per Saturday's steamers carrying steerage passengers, cabin, $80 gold; Steerage, $30 gold.

INMAN LINE.—Saturdays and Thursdays, from Pier No. 45, N. R., office 15 Broadway. Passage, First Cabin, $75 gold; Steerage, $30 currency.

NATIONAL LINE.—Saturdays from Pier No. 47, N. R., office 69 Broadway. Passage, $65 and $75, currency; Steerage, $28, currency.

LIVERPOOL AND GREAT WESTERN CO.—Wednesdays, from Pier No. 40, N. R., office 63 Wall street. Cabin Passage, $80, gold; Steerage, $30, currency.

WHITE STAR LINE.—Every Saturday from White Star Dock, Pavonia, Jersey City, office 19 Broadway. Cabin Passage, $80, gold; Steerage, $33, Currency.

FOR GLASGOW.

ANCHOR LINE.—Wednesdays and Saturdays from Pier 20, N. R., office No. 7 Bowling Green. Cabin Passage, $65 and $75; Steerage, $28, currency.

FOR HAVRE.

GENERAL TRANSATLANTIC COMPANY.—Saturdays from Pier No. 50, N. R., office No. 58 Broadway. Passage, 1st Cabin, $125; 2d, $75, gold, including wine.

FOR HAMBURG.

HAMBURG-AMERICAN PACKET COMPANY.—Wednesdays from Hoboken, office for passage, No. 6 Barclay street. Passage, First Cabin, adults, $120; Second Cabin, $72; Steerage, $30. Children and Servants at reduced rates.

FOR BREMEN.

NORTH GERMAN LLOYD STEAMSHIP COMPANY.—Days of sailing not regular. Eight or ten times per month, from Hoboken, office, 68 Broad street. Passage, First Cabin, $120; Second, $72; Steerage, $40.

FOR STETTIN.

BALTIC LLOYD MAIL STEAMSHIP COMPANY. Days of sailing, Saturdays, from Pier, 13, N. R., office, 40 Broadway. Cabin Passage, $80; Steerage, $30.

FOR BERMUDA.

Days of sailing, every third Thursday from Pier No. 21, N. R., office 54 Exchange place. Passage, $30, gold.

FOR ST. THOMAS, W. I., AND RIO JANEIRO

UNITED STATES AND BRAZIL MAIL STEAMSHIP COMPANY.—Days of sailing, the 23d of every month, from Pier No. 33. N. R., office, No. 5 Bowling Green. Passage to St. Thomas, $100; to Para, $150; to Pernambuco, $200; to Bahia, $210; to Rio Janeiro, $225. Children under 12 years, half price.

FOR ASPINWALL, via., Kingston, Jamaica, Panama South and Central American ports, China, and Japan.

THE PACIFIC STEAMSHIP COMPANY.—Sailing days, 15th and 30th of each month, from Pier 42, N. R. Passage to Kingston, Jamaica, $70 or $75, currency; Steerage, $35. To Aspinwall, $90 or $100, currency; Steerage, $41. To Panama, $25 gold additional. New York to San Francisco, $125 or $150, according to location of berth; Steerage, $60, currency. San Francisco, to Yokohama, $250 gold and $5 currency. To Hong Kong, Shanghai, Hiogo, or Nagasaki, $300 gold and $9 currency.

FOR HAVANA.

THE ATLANTIC MAIL STEAMSHIP COMPANY.—Calls at Nassau monthly. Days of sailing, Thursdays from Pier No. 4, N. R., office 5 Bowling Green. Fare to Havana on steamers Columbia and Moro Castle, $70, currency; on steamer Missouri, $60, currency. To Nassau, on all the steamers of the line, $50, gold.

NEW YORK AND MEXICAN S. S. COMPANY.—Every ten days from Pier 17, E. R., office 33 Broadway. Passage $65, currency.

FOR VERA CRUZ AND PROGRESO.

NEW YORK AND MEXICAN S. S. COMPANY.—Every twenty days from Pier 17, E. R., office, 33 Broadway. Passage to Progreso, $80, gold. To Vera Cruz, $100 gold, First Cabin; $60 Second Cabin.

MULTUM IN PARVO.

REDFIELD'S

AVELER'S GUIDE

TO THE

CITY OF NEW YORK

WITH A MAP.

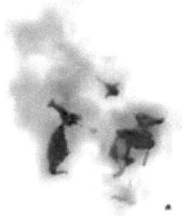

NEW YORK
J. S. REDFIELD, PUBLISHER
140 FULTON STREET
1871.

The Cheapest and most Complete Guide Book to the City.

PRICE 25 CENTS

Published by

J. S. REDFIELD,

140 Fulton Street, New York.

I. *Modern Women and What is Said of Them*: A Reprint of a Series of Articles in the *Saturday Review*, with an Introduction by Mrs. Lucia Gilbert Calhoun. *First Series.*

Contents—The Girl of the Period, Foolish Virgins, Little Women, Pinchbeck, Feminine Affectations, Ideal Women, Woman and the World, Unequal Marriages, Husband Hunting, Perils of "Paying Attention," Women's Heroines, Interference, Plain Girls, A Word for Female Vanity, The Abuse of Match-Making, Feminine Influence, Pigeons, Pretty Preachers, Ambitious Wives, Platonic Women, Man and his Master, The Goose and the Gander, Engagements, Woman in Orders, Woman and her Critics, Mistress and Maid, or Dress and Undress, Æsthetic Woman, What is Woman's Work? Papal Woman, Modern Mothers, Priesthood of Woman, The Future of Woman, La Femme Passée, The Fading Flower, Spoilt Women, Costume and its Morals.

In one Volume, 12mo, handsomely printed and bound in cloth, beveled boards, Price Two Dollars.

II. *Modern Women and What is Said of Them*: a Series of Articles Reprinted from *The Saturday Review*. *Second Series.*

Contents.—The Fashionable Woman, Man and his Disenchanter, Nymphs, Old Girls, Feminine Amenities, Grim Females, Widows, Charming Women, Apron-strings, Bored Husbands, Flattery, Arguing with Women, Women's Weapons, The Art of Coaxing, The Wild Women, Desœuvrement, Governesses, The Shrieking Sisterhood, Pretty Women, The Birch in the Boudoir, Pumpkins, The Social Lady-Bird, Buttercups, Beauty and Brains, Mésalliances, Weak Sisters, Semi-Detached Wives, Mature Sirens, Dolls, Dove Cotes, Fine Feelings, Flirting, Chaperons, First Love, Sweet Seventeen, Wasp Waists, Friendship, Shrews, Exclusiveness of Women, Popular Women, Men's Favorites, Womanliness, Falling in Love, The London Season.

In one vol., 12mo, 400 pp. Price Two Dollars.

III. *Conjugal Sins against the Laws of Life and Health*, and their Effects upon the Father, Mother and Child. By A. K. Gardner, A.M., M.D.

Contents.—The Modern Woman's Physical Deterioration; Local Disease in Children, and its Causes; At What Age should one Marry; Is Continence Physically Injurious? Personal Pollution; The Injurious Results of Physical Excess; Methods Used to Prevent Conception, and their Consequences; Infanticide; Conjugal Relations during the Period of Menstruation; Conjugal Relations between the Old; Marriage between Old Men and Young Girls; What may be Done with Health in View, and the Fear of God before us.

IV. ***Tribune Essays.*** Leading Articles contributed to *The New York Tribune*, from 1857 to 1863. By Charles T. Congdon, with an Introduction by Horace Greeley.

Contents.—Prefatory Notice, Introduction, Perils and Besetting Snares, Inaugural Glories, Mr. Benjamin Screws, Mr. Mason's Manners, The Great Rogersville Flogging, Mr. Mitchell's Desires, Mr. Mason's Manners Once More. Presidential Politeness, William the Conqueror, Benjamin's Second Notice. The Reveries of Reverdy, The Foresight of Mr., Fielder, Mr. Mitchell's Commercial Views, Father Ludovico's Fancy, Mr. Choate on Dr. Adams's Sermons, University Wanted. Mr. Pollard's "Mammy," A Church Going into Business, A New Laughing-Stock, A Cumberland Presbyterian Newspaper, Nil Nisi Bonum. Two Tombstones, The Perils of Pedagogy, Josiah's Jaunt, A Biographical Battle, Mr. Bancroft on the Declaration of Independence, Modern Chivalry—A Manifesto. Mr Fillmore takes a View, A Banner with a Strange Device, A Southern Diarist. Dr Tyler's Diagnosis. The Montgomery Muddle — A Specimen Day, Ready-made Unity and the Society for its Promotion, A Private Battery, Southern Notions of the North, Alexander the Bouncer, Roundheads and Cavaliers, Wise Convalescent Slaveholder's Honor, No Question before the House, Bella Molita—Soft War The Humanities South, The Charge of Precipitancy, The Assassination, Striking an Average. The Coming Despotism, Abolition and Secession, A Bacchanal of Beaufort, Concerning Shirts, Fair but Fierce. Bobbing Around, Niobe and Latona, Secession Squabbles, "Biblins," Cold Comfort, Extemporizing Production, Very Particular, Prudent Fugacity, Extemporizing Parties, Platform Novelties, Prophecies and Probabilities "Drawing it Mild" in Memphis, Loyalty and Light. Hedging, The Trial of Toombs. The Council of Thirty Five, Davis a Despot, All Means to Crush! Northern Independence, The Constitution—Not Conquest, Train's Troubles, The Slaveholding Utopia, Twelve Little Dirty Questions, Democracy in London, Laughter in New Hampshire, Slaveholding Virtues, Roland for an Oliver, Historical Scarecrows, The Other Way, Saulsbury's Sentiments, Jefferson the Gentleman, The Contagion of Secession, Davis to Mankind, Union for the Union, The Necessity of Servility, What shall we do with Them? Pocket Morality, Waiting for a Partner, At Home and Abroad, Mr. Davis proposes to Fast, Mr. B. Wood's Utopia, Mr. Buxton Scared, Charleston Cozy, The Twin Abominations, Victory and Victuals, Sus. Per Coll.

WALT. WHITMAN'S BOOKS.

V. ***Leaves of Grass.*** A new Edition, with additions and revisions. 1 vol. 12mo, paper. uncut $2.50.

VI. ***Passage to India.*** A Sequel to "Leaves of Grass." 1 vol. 12mo, paper, uncut. $1.00.

VII. ***Democratic Vistas*** (Prose). 1 vol. 12mo, paper, uncut. 75 cents.

VIII. ***On the Uses of Wines in Health and Disease.*** By Francis E. Anstie, M.D., F.R.C.P. Paper, 50 cts.

IX. *Modern Palmistry; or the Book of the* Hand. Chiefly according to the systems of D'Arpentigny and Desbarrolles, with some account of the Gipsies. By A. R. Craig, M. A., with illus. Cloth extra. $1.75.

Contents.—Palmistry as a Science, Ancient Palmistry, The Modern Science and its High-Priest, Signs attached to the Palm of the Hand, The Thumb, Hard and Soft Hands, The Hand in Children, The Spatuled Hand, English Hands, The North American Hand, The Artist Hand, The Useful Hand, Chinese Hands, The Hand of the Philosopher, The Hand Psychical, Mixed Hands, The Female Hand, M. Desbarrolles and the Advanced School, Palmistry in relation to the Future, The Three Worlds of Chiromancy, The Mounts and Lines, The Line of the Head, The Line of Life—of Saturn—of the Liver—of Venus, The Line of the Sun, The Rascette, The Seven Capital Sins, Power of Interpretation, The Astral Fluid, The Children of the Ruling Planets—their Characters, Readings of the Hands of Celebrated Men and Women, M. D'Arpentigny and the Gipsies—Mr. Borrow's Researches, Gipsy Chiromants, The Hand as affected by Marriage, Conclusion.

X. *Hand-Book of Progressive Philosophy.* By Edward Schiller. One vol. 12mo, extra cloth, $1.75.

XI. *The Kidney; its Structure, Functions* and Diseases. Bright's Disease; the Urine—its Constituents; Chemical tests for the various Diseases; their Symptoms and Treatment; adapted to popular comprehension. By Edward H. Dixon, M. D.   Paper, .25

XII. *The Lover's Library;* or Tales of Sentiment and Passion. A collection of Love Stories by the best authors.   Paper, .50

XIII. *Redfield's Half-Dime Vest-Pocket City* Maps. New York City, now ready.   .05

XIV. *Little-Breeches.* By John Hay, Illustrated by J. T. Engel and photolithographed by the American Photolithographic Co. (Osborn's Process.)   .25

www.ingramcontent.com/pod-product-compliance
Lightning Source LLC
Chambersburg PA
CBHW030405170426
43202CB00010B/1492